THA

GAME CHANGÁ

FOOD, FITNESS, MOTIVATION

Fuel your body,
Empower your mind-
Through food, fitness
and motivation.

HORACE JONES

FIRST EDITION

ISBN: 978-1-7393670-0-8 (paperback)

Tha Game Changá by Horace Jones is published by TC Publishing

For information please direct emails to: info@ibelieveican.co.uk

TC PUBLISHING

Welcome to your

GAME-CHANGING MOMENT.

It only takes a moment to

change the game.

CONTENTS

From the desk of the Author 6

Introduction 7

Meal 1: Super Cabbage 11

Meal 2: Stuffed Peppers 19

Meal 3: Sweet Potato Deluxe 25

Meal 4: Energy Pasta 33

Meal 5: Delicious Pasta 43

Meal 6: Game Changá Pasta 49

Meal 7: Healing Dish Chickpeas 56

Meal 8: Tropical Flavours Cashew Nuts 63

Meal 9: Healthy Quinoa 71

Meal 10: Pumpkin Masala 78

Meal 11: Butter Beans & Sweet Potato 86

Meal 12: Mixed Bean Salad 92

Meal 13: Morning Wake Up 99

Meal 14: Sunshine Wake up 106

Meal 15: Super Heart Health 115

About the author 127

FROM THE DESK
OF THE AUTHOR

First, I want to say thank you for purchasing this book. I had a dream and was able to see it through, this is a wonderful feeling. I had an idea, but it took other people to bring it to life. For that, I'd like to thank Val Nowak and Richard G Davis.

On this journey of a million miles, you need to have great people around you. We all have dreams and ideas but sometimes we can't seem to bring them alive. With life's ups and downs and our discipline not being where it needs to be, our dream and goals seem to be so far away.

Our dreams have the power to come to fruition, when our paths cross with people who can support the missing pieces, we can help bring our dreams and goals into reality. We have been told not to tell people our ideas because they might take them. At the same time, we are told people will put us down. This book wouldn't have existed without support from other people.

My passion for cooking has always been there but I guess I didn't believe that I could have turned this idea into a tangible product. This idea has grown and included other areas of Fitness and Mental Well-Being through Motivation.

Finally, I want to say thank you to Les Brown, an international motivational speaker who I adopted as my mentor from a distance and who changed the game for me in a moment.

Horace "Game Changá" Jones

INTRODUCTION

VAL NOWAK &
HORACE JONES

Before I start, I would like to say thank you to myself for taking up the challenge of bettering and improving myself.

This book was put together by faith, the power of meeting people and opportunities. I met Val through a client from my fitness coaching class, that they had attended in Alexandra Park, Manchester, UK. Upon meeting Val, he inspired me to start seeing myself in a different light. Over a few Sundays, as a videographer for Vibe Media, Val saw my potential and was able to show me how to expand, expose and promote myself better in addition to adding content to his social media platform. This was wonderful news for me as I have been trying to promote myself but wasn't having any success.

A few weeks went by and our collaboration in the form of a fitness coaching video was shot, edited, and produced. Val sent me a link to the video, and I loved it! For the first time, I viewed myself as a professional. As our relationship grew, Val learned that I was a vegetarian which was challenging for him regarding what to cook. With gratitude for the fitness video, I offered to show Val firsthand in his own kitchen and cook him a few recipes. This continued to lead to an offer by Val to other platforms: Vibe Sports and Vibe Food. This was an opportunity I couldn't let pass so I took up the offer.

After a few weeks, we started to cook on the Vibe platform. Seeing myself on the big screen gave me a warm feeling inside that I haven't felt in a very long time. A few months went by, and we produced more than 10 recipes in HD video format. This all started with a conversation and being ready to take up an opportunity that was in front of me.

A big thank you to Val and Vibe Media for all the good work for the community of Manchester, United Kingdom.

I believe that you meet people for a reason. Richard wow, this guy came into my life when I was at a crossroads. As a friend of my Mum's, Richard and I spoke one or two times via phone, but I guess it wasn't our time to go on our journey. Years went by before we found something in common: Financial Literacy. It kicked off with Richard sending me information about cryptocurrency. I had no idea what it was but I was willing to learn. I remember like it was yesterday; on a Facebook Messenger call Richard said, "I can send you information on crypto but are you interested?" I said, "Yes. I don't understand it, but I want to learn." Then the friendship began.

Richard was the mentor and coach that I needed at that time in my life to give me the crossover that I was looking for. Meeting Richard opened my eyes to bigger and better opportunities. Can meeting someone really change your game? Yes. I am what you call living proof. People come into your life when you need them, but you must recognise what it is for, and have a vision of where you could be in a year with these new people around you and the opportunities presented.

I told Richard about what I do; cook a healthy meal for £5.00 that feeds 2.5 people, Fitness Coaching and an Outreach Motivational Coach for Teens and Adults. Then he started to engage idea after idea as it pertained to Food, Fitness and Motivation. I just ran with it! Before I knew it, I was inspired to build a profitable financial portfolio, host a Facebook Live Show, and write this book to continue my goal of helping 1 Billon people on a journey of personal Well Being.

Meeting these two people in my life gave me more confidence which made me visualise and believe, and with time I knew anything was possible.

A 'Game Changá' moment will be sent to you. It is up to you to find the time to listen, learn and better yourself along the way to personal well-being.

Horace Jones & Richard G. Davis

HOW TO USE **THIS BOOK**

Congratulations on taking the first step towards enhancing your overall well-being with "Tha Game Changá"!

Here's how to make the most of this revolutionary book:

Get motivated: Start by reading through the author's personal experiences and how they were able to transform their life through chance encounters and seizing opportunities. Let their story inspire you to make positive changes in your own life.

Dive into the recipes: The author shares a variety of mouth-watering vegetarian recipes that are not only delicious but also great for your health. Pick a few recipes that appeal to you and give them a try. Don't be afraid to experiment and make them your own.

Incorporate fitness routines: Along with the recipes, the author also shares effective and easy-to-follow fitness routines that can help improve your physical health. Choose a routine that fits your schedule and fitness level and stick to it consistently.

Track your progress: Keep track of your progress in a journal or planner. Write down any changes you notice in your physical health, mental well-being, and overall happiness. Celebrate your successes and use any setbacks as an opportunity to learn and grow.

Stay motivated: Use the author's personal anecdotes and inspirational quotes throughout the book to stay motivated and focused on your goals. Remember, 'Tha Game Changá' is not just a cookbook or a fitness guide – it is a comprehensive guide to transforming your life for the better. With dedication and consistency, you can achieve your goals and become the best version of yourself. It only takes a minute to change the game.

SUPER CABBAGE

History

The main ingredient of this dish goes from as Far East in North China where it was cultivated since 4000 BC. In Rome cabbage was considered a luxury and many regarded it as better than all other vegetables. They also used it for medicinal purposes as relief from gout to headaches.

Major Benefits

Cabbage is an exceptionally healthy food. It has an outstanding nutrient profile and is especially high in Vitamin C and K. It has positive effects on the body and organs. In addition, eating cabbage may even help lower the risk of certain diseases, improve digestion, and combat inflammation. It keeps blood pressure low, is anti-inflammatory, aids in weight loss, and is cancer preventative. It also helps to prevent osteoporosis by strengthening bones. It is good for stimulating the brain, and good for eye health.

Cabbage is a good source of vitamins A, B6, C, E, and K, Potassium, Magnesium, Calcium, Protein, Fiber, Folate, Iron, and Riboflavin.

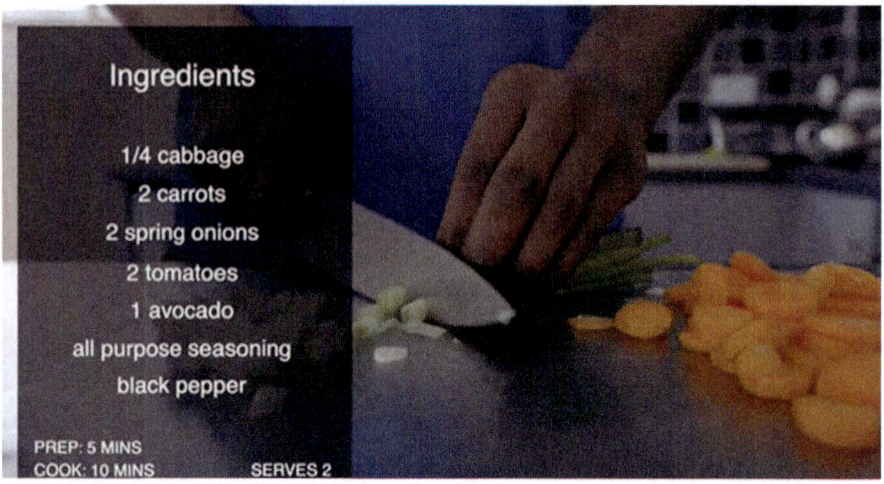

Instructions

In a large mixing bowl, combine shredded cabbage, grated carrots, and sliced spring onions.

Add diced tomatoes and diced avocado to the bowl, and gently toss the vegetables together.

Season the slaw with all-purpose seasoning and black pepper to taste, and continue tossing until the vegetables are evenly coated.

Serve the slaw immediately, garnished with extra sliced spring onions or chopped fresh herbs if desired.

Enjoy your healthy and flavourful cabbage slaw, perfect as a side dish or a light lunch!

FITNESS SESSION: 1

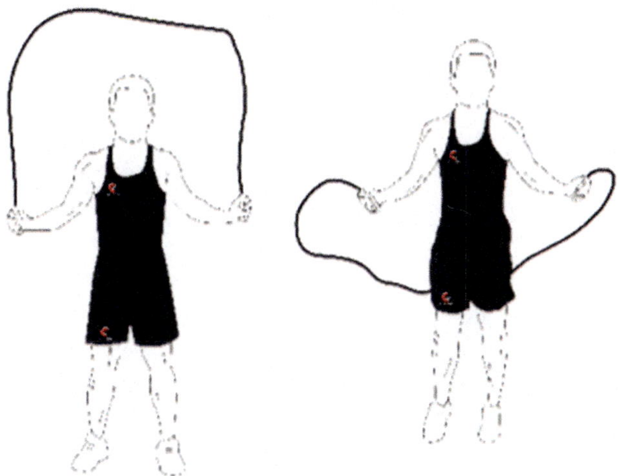

Target Area: Whole-body workout

When beginning a fitness plan, it is important to consult your doctor if you have medical issues and start at a moderate pace. Always stretch before any exercise. Walking is best until you feel strong enough to Jog or Run. Also, have a little fun and try Skipping or Riding a Bike. Be sure to consult your doctor before adopting any form of exercise plan. (Yes, we did repeat ourselves ☺)

Start off with a warm-up of stretches which should take approximately 15 minutes.

1 Push-up
1 Burpee
1 Tuck jump
10 Squat
10 seconds Sprint on the spot

This exercise is a pyramid sequence to test your level of fitness by starting light and increasing every time. For example, round one is one of each exercise then is followed by round two which is two of each exercise. 10 squats and 10 seconds of sprinting on the spot after every set.

Warm-up and Stretches:

Shoulder Rolls: Roll your shoulders forward in a circular motion, and then roll them backwards for 30 seconds.

Arm Swings: Stand with your feet shoulder-width apart, and swing your arms back and forth for 30 seconds.

Leg Swings: Stand on one leg and swing the other leg back and forth, then switch to the other leg and repeat for 30 seconds.

Torso Twists: Stand with your feet shoulder-width apart and twist your torso to the left and right for 30 seconds.

Hamstring Stretches: Stand with your feet shoulder-width apart and reach down to touch your toes. Hold for 30 seconds.

Round 1: 1 Push-up, 1 Burpee, 1 Tuck jump, 10 Squats, 10 Push-ups. After completing each set of exercises, take a 30 second break and move on to the next round.

Start with 1 push-up: Begin in a plank position with your hands shoulder-width apart, core engaged, and back straight. Lower your body until your chest touches the floor, then push back up to the starting position. Repeat for one rep.

Add 1 burpee: From a standing position, jump up and land in a squat position with your hands on the ground. Kick your feet back to a plank position, perform a push-up, then jump your feet back to the squat position and stand up. Repeat for one rep.

Add 1 tuck jump: Start in a standing position, then jump as high as you can while bringing your knees up towards your chest. Land softly and repeat for one rep.

Add 10 squats. Stand with your feet shoulder-width apart, bend your knees, and lower your hips down as if you are sitting in a chair.

Add 10 seconds of sprinting on the spot: Run on the spot as fast as you can for 10 seconds.

Repeat the entire sequence, adding one rep to each of the first three exercises, until you reach your desired number of reps or time limit. Make sure to rest as needed and hydrate throughout the workout.

Round 2: 2 Push-ups, 2 Burpees, 2 Tuck jumps, 10 x Squats, 10 Push-ups

Round 3: 3 Push-ups, 3 Burpees, 3 Tuck jumps, 10 Squats, 10 Push-ups

Continue adding one repetition to each exercise until you reach your personal best. Make sure to take a 30 second break between each set of exercises to allow your muscles to recover.

Warm-Down: After completing the pyramid sequence exercise, it is important to cool down and stretch your muscles to prevent injury and reduce muscle soreness. This cool-down routine should take approximately 5-10 minutes.

1-2 minutes of walking
1-2 minutes of slow jogging
1-2 minutes of static stretching for each muscle group, including hamstrings, quads, calves, hip flexors, and shoulders.

Remember to listen to your body and adjust the exercises as necessary to prevent injury. Consult with a doctor or fitness professional before starting any new exercise routine, especially if you have any pre-existing medical conditions or injuries.

Motivation: Discipline

For most of my life, I have seen the word discipline as a reflection of behaviour. Now that I am grown, I see that to really achieve the best in one's self is to be disciplined. We all have greatness inside of us. However, being side-tracked and day-to-day life makes us blind which moves our focus elsewhere. We must look at discipline as a good thing, for us to shine like a diamond and be disciplined long enough so change can happen.

Running a race with no direction is no different from walking backwards. To make every single step count you must have a goal. Growing up, the whole concept of discipline was what you can't do. There wasn't any understanding that if I could discipline myself, I could become the higher me. I couldn't see the benefits of discipline. The few role models that I had were not showing me much. Apart from holding down a job that they didn't want, everyone seemed to be waiting for the weekend so that they could run away from their life. Discipline showed up all through my life as a young boy who didn't understand its importance, to becoming a man who swears by it.

Looking back now I can see that from a young age I had to be disciplined, I just didn't know this was what discipline meant. I grew up with very little. At times I had to stay with family who had their own children and responsibilities, so funds were very hard to come by. How I learned to save was discipline in disguise. When I was a child the best way to make money was every time there was a football match, I'm talking 1990s when Manchester City's football club was based in Moss-Side. Man City played at home every two weeks. We called it 'minding cars.' In those days, attendees of the football match paid children to watch their cars whilst they attended the match. For every young boy, this was an opportunity to make some good pocket money. The only thing was you had to be quick at running. Being faster than everyone gave you an edge. You also had to have the eyesight of an eagle.

It showed me over time that I had to be disciplined with my money. I learned how to break down my money from buying sweets to buying little toys then making sure there was enough to last until the next football match.

My passion for the gym started in my early 20s. I loved the gym more than anything. I was mostly training with people that were much older than I and making time and keeping to a schedule was important. The routine was carved in stone; 3 times a week, no matter what. No making up any excuses because you couldn't make it. All these things were teaching me discipline, but I just didn't see it as discipline. It was just something we did. I couldn't see at the time how discipline was shaping my life and I just took it as nothing. Sometimes life can alter things and the discipline that you found so easily seems so far away. But remember that you once had it. Everything comes down to time and your desire for what you want.

I choose discipline over motivation any day of the week. Motivation will come and go but when you are disciplined about something, it takes a lot to push you off track. Just like anything you have to work at it. With consistency and time and you will be amazed at the results. From learning how to save money to training my body in weightlifting and Thai boxing, and working 3 jobs. All these things take discipline and the rewards are worth it.

“

Discipline is the bridge between goals and accomplishment.

-Jim Rohn

STUFFED "POWER" PEPPERS

History

Like their relatives the chili peppers, bell peppers originated in South America with seeds of a wild variety dating back to 5000 BC. They span the globe as Spanish and Portuguese explorers travelled the world sharing the richness of these foods uncommon to their region.

Major Benefits

Bell Peppers are a great source of Vitamin A which is important for vision. It also helps the heart, lungs, and kidneys. Natural potassium helps your muscles work including the muscles that control your heartbeat and breathing.

The Bell Pepper alone has Vitamins A, B, C, E, and K. Its mineral content consists of Potassium, Magnesium, Iron, Phosphorus, and Copper.

Instructions:

Preheat the oven to 375°F (190°C).

Cut the tops off the bell peppers and remove the seeds and membranes from the inside. Place the bell peppers in a baking dish.

In a large pan over medium heat, add a splash of oil and sauté the diced eggplant, butternut squash, sliced mushrooms, and sliced spring onions until they are slightly softened and browned for about 8-10 minutes.

Add the sliced okra to the pan and sauté for another 2-3 minutes.

While the vegetables are cooking, cook the couscous according to the package instructions.

Once the vegetables are cooked, stir in the cooked couscous and season with all-purpose seasoning and black pepper to taste.

Stuff the bell peppers with the couscous and vegetable mixture, packing it down tightly.

Place the stuffed bell peppers in the preheated oven and bake for 25-30 minutes, or until the peppers are tender and the filling is heated through.

Serve hot and enjoy your delicious stuffed peppers!

Note: You can also add some grated cheese to the top of the stuffed peppers before baking for an extra tasty and melty touch.

FITNESS SESSION: 2

Target area: Whole-body workout

Warm-up your body with the exercises from the previous session.

Push-ups: reps of 10 x 3 sets

Sit-ups: reps of 10 x 3 sets

Dips: reps of 10 x 3 sets

Sumo Squats (legs wide): reps of 10 x 3 sets

Lunges (alternate legs): reps of 10 x 3 sets

Mountain Climbers: reps of 10 x 3 sets All exercises are reps of 10 x 3 sets

Don't forget to warm-down. Stretches are important to start your workout and finish your workout.

Push-ups: Start with a plank position, with your hands slightly wider than shoulder-width apart. Lower your body towards the ground, keeping your elbows close to your body. Push back up to the starting position, keeping your core engaged. Repeat for 10 reps, for 3 sets. **Sit-ups:** Lay down on your back with your knees bent and feet on the ground. Place your hands behind your head, keeping your elbows wide. Engage your core and lift your upper body towards your knees. Lower back down slowly, keeping your core engaged. Repeat for 10 reps, for 3 sets.

Dips: Find a bench or chair and sit on the edge with your hands placed next to your hips. Lower your body towards the ground by bending your elbows, keeping them close to your body. Push back up to the starting position. Repeat for 10 reps, for 3 sets.

Sumo Squats: Start with your feet wider than hip-width apart, with your toes pointed outwards. Lower your body down into a squat, keeping your back straight. Push back up to the starting position, squeezing your glutes. Repeat for 10 reps, for 3 sets.

Lunges: Start with your feet hip-width apart. Step forward with one leg, bending both knees to form a lunge. Push back up to the starting position, alternating legs. Repeat for 10 reps on each leg, for 3 sets.

Mountain Climbers: Start in a plank position, with your hands shoulder-width apart. Bring your right knee towards your chest, then switch to your left knee. Repeat in a quick, alternating motion for 10 reps, for 3 sets.

Warm-down stretches:

Hamstring stretch: sit on the ground with your legs straight out in front of you. Reach forward towards your toes, keeping your back straight.

Quadriceps stretch: stand up straight and bring your right heel towards your glute, holding onto your ankle with your right hand. Keep your left arm out for balance.

Shoulder stretch: bring your right arm across your chest and hold it with your left hand. Repeat with your left arm.

Triceps stretch: reach your right arm up and bend it at the elbow, reaching your right hand down your back. Hold onto your right elbow with your left hand. Repeat with your left arm.

Remember to listen to your body and adjust the exercises as necessary to prevent injury. Consult with a doctor or fitness professional before starting any new exercise routine, especially if you have any pre-existing medical conditions or injuries.

Motivation: The First Step

I bought a picture a few years back because of the inspiring words of a Chinese proverb that was written on it. It read; "A journey of a thousand miles begins with a single step." We all have our journeys to go on but find it difficult to make that first step. The magic starts when we step out of our comfort zone. Under uncomfortable conditions of pressure, carbonated rocks become a diamond. It goes through several stages over many years. See yourself as a diamond and with time you will have the finished product you are looking for. The key to this is to visualize yourself. It will happen and give yourself time like the diamond.

Another saying that motivates me says, "If you want something you've never had, you must be willing to do something you've never done before." - Thomas Jefferson. This is easier said than done. My childhood seemed to be full of failures even though I wasn't really scared of trying new things. I guess it was more about my comfort zone. One of the hardest things in life is change. We don't want to see it but sometimes it is an absolute necessity. It may take a life and death experience or even the doctors telling you if you don't change your habits you're going to die.

Why do some of us tend to live our lives this way? Change may be the best thing for us but we ignore it for the (bad) habits that we have picked up along the way. The most rewarding thing that I have done is wanting change and being honest enough to take that first step. We fear the unknown. That is why most of us don't try anything new. The only thing that we are guaranteed is death so why not take a chance and go for the change? I took that chance and made that change because if you just do what is easy your life will be hard. So, the key is to do what is hard to have an easy life.

What does the first step look like? Well in my experience it starts with hardship, worry, anxiety, people not believing in you, and self-doubt. It is hard work so I can see why a lot of people don't want to change. But some things are worth fighting for, to change for the better and to really experience the better version of yourself. What could be more exhilarating than that? Or do you want to wait until you're on your death bed by then it will be too late? To achieve anything in life you have to take that first step. After that, it is all about consistency.

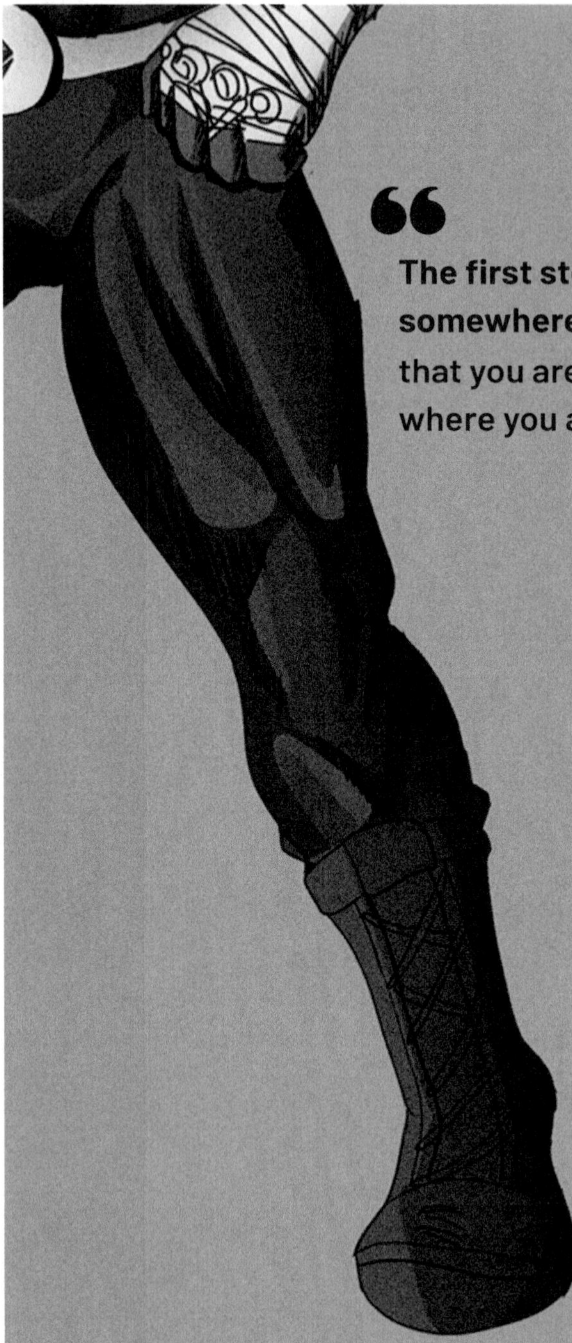

> “
> **The first step toward getting somewhere is to decide**
> that you are not going to stay where you are.
>
> *- Chauncey Depew*

SWEET POTATO DELUXE

History

Sweet potatoes originated in Central and South America. But archaeologists have found prehistoric remnants of sweet potatoes in Polynesia from about A.D. 1000 to A.D. 1100, according to radiocarbon dating. They've hypothesized that those ancient samples came from the western coast of South America

Major Benefits:

Sweet potatoes have surprising health benefits. They are highly nutritious and are a great source of fibre, vitamins, and minerals. They promote gut health, may have cancer-fighting properties, and support healthy vision. They may also enhance brain function, and support your immune system.

Sweet potatoes contain the following: Vitamin A which is necessary for healthy eyes and skin, Vitamin C for healthy nerves and immune system, and Vitamin B6 to aid metabolism and form red blood cells.

Sweet potatoes are also full of calcium and potassium, which aids bone strength, muscle function, and heart function.

Instructions:

Preheat the oven to 200°C (400°F).

In a large bowl, mix the sweet potato cubes with some olive oil, salt, black pepper, and all-purpose seasoning until well coated.

Spread the sweet potato cubes in a single layer on a baking sheet and roast in the preheated oven for about 20-25 minutes or until they are tender and lightly browned.

In the meantime, mix the eggplant cubes with some olive oil, salt, black pepper, and all-purpose seasoning until well coated.

Spread the eggplant cubes in a single layer on another baking sheet and roast in the preheated oven for about 15-20 minutes or until they are tender and lightly browned.

Cut the red onion into wedges and mix with some olive oil, salt, black pepper, and all-purpose seasoning until well coated.

Add the red onion wedges to the eggplant baking sheet and roast for another 10 minutes or until the onion wedges are tender and lightly browned.

In the last few minutes of roasting, add the asparagus to the sweet potato baking sheet and roast for about 5-7 minutes or until the asparagus is tender and lightly browned.

Once everything is roasted, combine the sweet potato cubes, eggplant cubes, red onion wedges, and asparagus in a large bowl.

Add the chopped lettuce and toss everything together. Season with more salt, black pepper, and all-purpose seasoning to taste.

Serve warm and enjoy!

Fitness Session: 3

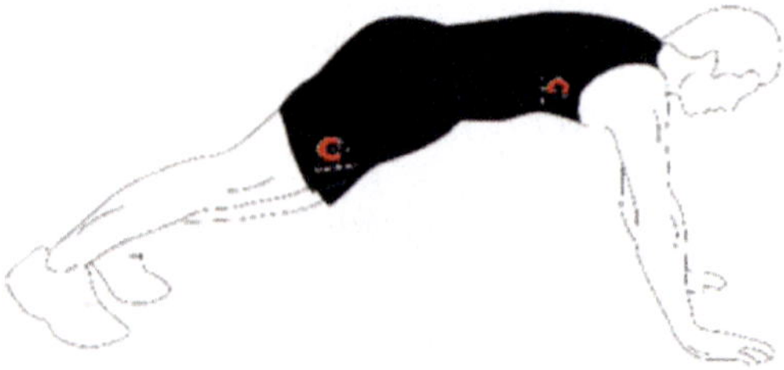

Target area: Shoulders, abs and legs.

Warm-up and Stretches: 5-10 minutes

Push-ups: 10 x 3

Mountain climbers: 10 x 3

Squat thrusts: 10 x 3

Shoulder taps: 10 x 3

Walk-out push-ups: 10 x 3

Warm-down and stretch.

Warm-up and Stretches: Start with some light cardio exercises such as jumping jacks or jogging in place for 2-3 minutes. Follow this with stretches for your legs, arms, shoulders, back and neck to increase flexibility and reduce the risk of injury.

Push-ups: Start in a high plank position with your hands shoulder-width apart and your feet hip-width apart. Lower your body down towards the ground until your chest almost touches the ground, then push yourself back up to the starting position. Repeat this motion for 10 repetitions, for 3 sets.

Mountain climbers: Begin in a high plank position with your hands shoulder-width apart and your feet hip-width apart. Bring one knee towards your chest, then quickly switch to bring the other knee towards your chest. Repeat this motion as fast as you can for 10 repetitions, for 3 sets.

Squat thrust: Stand with your feet hip-width apart. Squat down and place your hands on the ground in front of you, then jump your feet back to come into a high plank position. Quickly jump your feet forward towards your hands and then stand up to return to the starting position. Repeat this motion for 10 repetitions, for 3 sets.

Shoulder taps: Start in a high plank position with your hands shoulder-width apart. Lift one hand off the ground and tap the opposite shoulder, then place the hand back on the ground. Repeat this motion with the other hand. Continue alternating shoulder taps for 10 repetitions, for 3 sets.

Walk-out push-ups: Stand with your feet hip-width apart. Bend forward and place your hands on the ground, then walk your hands out until you're in a high plank position. Do one push-up, then walk your hands back towards your feet and stand up to return to the starting position. Repeat this motion for 10 repetitions, for 3 sets.

Warm-down and Stretch: Finish the session with some light cardio exercises such as walking or jogging in place for 2-3 minutes. Then, do stretches for your legs, arms, shoulders, back and neck to reduce muscle tension and improve flexibility.

Remember to stay hydrated throughout the workout and listen to your body. If you experience any pain or discomfort, stop the exercise and consult a healthcare professional.

Motivation: 50, 30, 20 Rule

For as long as I can remember, I have always been exceptionally good at saving money. I guess when you have no choice you learn to adapt very quickly. I'm sure some of us started working at a very early stage in our lives. It was only later in my life that I saw the true value of being able to put a little away every month. It was not long before I developed the '50, 30, 20 rule'

Starting with a nice small number of 100£, let us say all your living expenses like bills are around 30£ .50£ for food, entertainment and others. You must keep to this budget no matter what. Even if you run out before your next payday. That leaves 20£ which is your investment and saving money. It is the same with 2000£. Always make sure you put away 20 percent of your wages as savings and investments. Being able to put something away for a rainy day is key to growth. However, the next level of growth is to give your money a job. The plan is to save eight times your salary by the time you are 60 years old.

Look at investing in yourself first then in other opportunities like Real Estate, Stocks, FX, and Crypto Currency. The key is really to spend less on luxury and material things and try to save your party money. Journaling your spending, saving and investments along with having a target will keep you focused. In time, you want to match your savings and investments and in a longer time frame the investments exceed your savings exponentially. The first one or two months may seem difficult but with sacrifice, you will master this. You must train your mind to look towards the future in an instant-gratification society.

Some of us get caught up in the latest fashion or gadgets, which entails taking our money. The system is designed to take our money in all kinds of ways from having a home, to all the bills you have to pay to maintain a car, hobbies, habits, children, and the list goes on. Sometimes we find we find ourselves with two jobs and still can't cut it. So, what do you do?

For me, most things came down to sacrifice. Living within one's means does not mean you can't have nice things or go out for a meal. It just means I learned from a very young age, how to divide my money. I had no choice but to do so, with no parents around most of my life. The little money that I came by had to last mainly because I didn't know when I might have more. As I got older, having a home and child to provide for, more money had to come in, so I got myself another job or did overtime when it was available. My mindset was to always try and put a little bit away, no matter what. I read a book that just installed itself in my head like cement and this is where I got the '50, 30, 20 rule' from. The most important part to me was the saving part; the rule was no matter what I had to find that 20% to put away. I remember one morning I woke up to my boiler and washing machine not working. What saved me was the savings that I had put away.

The key to this was to never spend more than your 30% which was your social money; going for food, nights out, buying clothes, shoes or whatever you fancy. The reason for this was that your 50% breakdown towards bills is something that you couldn't really change. The only money that you had to play with was your 30%. If you went over that it meant you were now dipping into your 20% savings.

This is where most of us go wrong and why we can never seem to save enough to really make a difference in our lives. It comes down to discipline and sacrifice. It is up to you to decide on the amount you put away each week or month. But remember this we will always find the money for what we want to find it for.

“

You have to learn the rules of the game, and then you have to play better than anyone else.

- Albert Einstein

ENERGY PASTA

History:

The cherry tomato is believed to be the direct ancestor of modern cultivated tomatoes and is the only wild tomato found outside South America. The tomato is thought to have been first domesticated in the Puebla-Veracruz area of Mexico and to have reached this area from South America in the form of a weedy cherry tomato. The first direct reference to the cherry tomato appears in 1623, in a work called *Pinax theatri botanici* (English: *Illustrated exposition of plants*) by Swiss botanist Caspar Bauhin, which contains descriptions and classifications of approximately six thousand species. In a section on "Solanum" (nightshades), Bauhin wrote of a variety called *Solanum racemosum cerasoru[m] forma*, which translates to "Solanum [that is] full of clusters [racemosum], in the form (shape) of cherries." Cherry tomatoes have been popular in the United States since at least 1919. Recipes using cherry tomatoes can be found in articles dating back to 1967.

Major Benefits:

Cherry tomatoes are rich in lycopene, which is great at fighting the free radicals that cause disease. Lycopene can also limit UV damage to your skin from sun exposure and promote better heart health.

Cherry tomatoes are also an excellent source of Potassium, Vitamin A, Vitamin C, and Vitamin E.

Instructions:

Bring a large pot of salted water to a boil. Add the pasta and cook according to the package instructions, until al dente.

While the pasta is cooking, chop the broccoli into small florets, dice the red onion, and slice the spring onions.

Heat some oil in a pan over medium heat. Add the red onion and cook for a few minutes until softened.

Add the broccoli to the pan and continue to cook for a few minutes until tender. Add the cherry tomatoes and cook for a further minute.

Drain the cooked pasta and add it to the pan with the vegetables. Stir to combine.

Add the green pesto to the pan and stir through the pasta and vegetables until everything is well coated.

Season with salt and black pepper to taste.

Serve hot, garnished with sliced spring onions. Enjoy!

Fitness Session: 4

Target area: Fat burner, Core

Warm-up and stretches: 5-10 minutes

High knees: 45 seconds
Low plank to high plank: 45 seconds **Crunches:** 45 seconds
Mountain climbers: 45 seconds **Half-burpees:** 45 seconds
Walk-out push-ups: 45 seconds

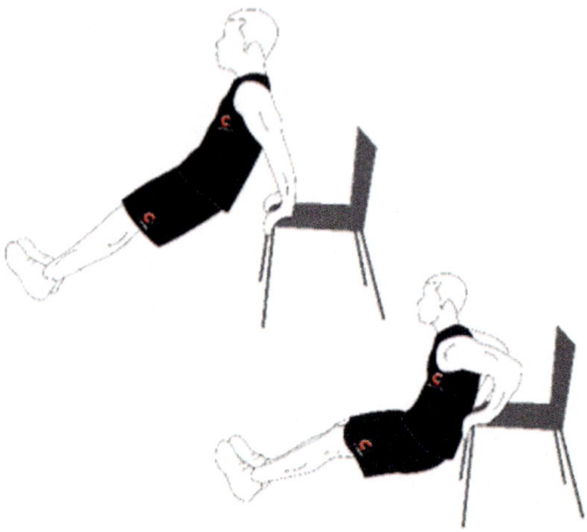

Each exercise is 45 seconds and 15 seconds rest.

Finish off with warm-down and stretching exercises.

Warm-up and Stretches: Begin your workout with the following warm-up exercises.

Shoulder Rolls: Roll your shoulders forward in a circular motion, and then roll them backwards for 30 seconds.

Arm Swings: Stand with your feet shoulder-width apart and swing your arms back and forth for 30 seconds.

Leg Swings: Stand on one leg and swing the other leg back and forth, then switch to the other leg and repeat for 30 seconds.

Torso Twists: Stand with your feet shoulder-width apart and twist your torso to the left and right for 30 seconds.

Hamstring Stretches: Stand with your feet shoulder-width apart and reach down to touch your toes. Hold for 30 seconds.

High knees: Stand with your feet shoulder-width apart and lift your knees as high as you can for 45 seconds. Rest for 15 seconds.

Low Plank to high plank: Start in a low plank position with your elbows on the ground, then push-up into a high plank position, one arm at a time. Alternate between low and high plank for 45 seconds. Rest for 15 seconds.

Crunches: Lie on your back with your knees bent and your feet flat on the ground. Place your hands behind your head and lift your shoulders off the ground for 45 seconds. Rest for 15 seconds.

Mountain Climbers: Start in a high plank position and bring your right knee to your chest, then switch to your left knee. Alternate between your right and left knee for 45 seconds. Rest for 15 seconds.

Half-burpees: Stand with your feet shoulder-width apart, then squat down and place your hands on the ground. Kick your feet back into a plank position, then jump your feet back to your hands and stand up. Repeat for 45 seconds. Rest for 15 seconds.

Walk-out push-ups: Start standing up, then reach down to touch your toes and walk your hands out into a high plank position. Do one push-up, then walk your hands back to your feet and stand up. Repeat for 45 seconds. Rest for 15 seconds.

Push-ups: Start in a high plank position with your hands shoulder-width apart, then lower your body until your chest touches the ground. Push yourself back up and repeat for 45 seconds. Rest for 15 seconds.

Remember, each exercise is 45 seconds with 15 seconds of rest in between.

Warm-down and Stretches: Now that the workout is complete, take a few minutes to cool down and stretch out your muscles.

Shoulder Stretch: Stand with your feet shoulder-width apart and clasp your hands behind your back. Lift your arms up and stretch for 30 seconds.

Quad Stretch: Stand with your feet shoulder-width apart and lift your right foot towards your buttocks. Hold onto your ankle and stretch for 30 seconds, then switch legs and repeat.

Hamstring Stretch: Sit on the ground with your legs stretched out in front of you. Reach forward and touch your toes, holding for 30 seconds.

Butterfly Stretch: Sit on the ground with the soles of your feet touching each other. Hold onto your ankles and gently push your knees towards the ground for 30 seconds.

Remember to stay hydrated throughout the workout. Listen to your body and take breaks when needed. If you experience any pain or discomfort, stop the exercise and consult a healthcare professional.

Motivation: Change-Fixed-Growth

Life is a process of ups and downs. As the saying goes; "Life is 10% of what happens to you and 90% of how you react to it." - Charles R. Swindoll. If you are tired of being where you are in life or unsatisfied with results, start with a change of mindset. Patience is a must. You have to give yourself long enough for something to change or start working. Jumping from one thing to another or changing your mind at every second will defeat the long-term positive results for momentary satisfaction.

A Change Mindset refers to a shift or transformation in a person's way of thinking and perceiving the world around them. It involves adopting a new perspective, beliefs, values, and attitudes that can significantly impact how a person approaches various aspects of life, such as personal growth, relationships, work, and overall well-being. A Change mindset can be positive or negative, depending on the nature of the shift. Overall, a Change mindset can have a significant impact on a person's life, influencing their behaviour, emotions, and overall quality of life. It can lead to personal growth, increased resilience, and a more positive outlook on life.

A Fixed Mindset is a belief that one's abilities, intelligence, and personal characteristics are largely fixed and cannot be changed. Individuals with a fixed mindset tend to believe that their traits are predetermined and cannot be improved through effort, practice, or learning. Having a Fixed mindset can limit your potential and prevent personal growth, as individuals may avoid taking risks or trying new things for fear of failure.

A positive change in mindset could involve developing a Growth Mindset, which emphasises the belief that one's abilities and intelligence can be developed through dedication and hard work. This type of mindset can lead to increased motivation, resilience, and perseverance in the face of challenges. All 3 mindsets have their purpose. You only have to figure out when to act on each one.

Stubborn; strong-minded; and prideful: These are some of the qualities that go with having a Fixed mindset set at the wrong time. Now the key is knowing when to use a Fixed mindset to your advantage. This mindset can sometimes get in the way of progress due to pride when we don't want to look like we are wrong. As an advantage, the best time to have a mindset is when you are working towards something like fitness goals, education, or a skill to improve yourself.

With a productive Changed and Fixed mindset, the outcome is a Growth mindset. You arrive at a point of willingness to learn new things, take on creative ideas and work with people with the same optimistic mindset. Those that have Growth mindsets are those that are willing to read that book, get that course done and never give up until they achieve their goals and targets.

Knowing when to implement a Growth mindset or having a Fixed mindset about something or even a Changed mindset doesn't come easy. I found myself in my younger years only going between having a Fixed mindset and a Change mindset. When I say a Fixed mindset I'm talking about how you deal with day-to-day problems, Relationships, Tasks, and inner thoughts. I seemed to be dealing with my problems the same way but expecting a different outcome. My attitude toward life was the same for a very long time. My environment was impacted blindly which seemed to lead me to have no change in my life. In a Change mindset, it was never knowing what I wanted, always jumping from one thing to another. I never had a plan. The only plan if I had one at all was survival.

The Growth mindset came later in my journey. This is where I can say my attitude changed towards life. I guess I stopped blaming others for my mishaps, my past, my trauma. You can't have a growth mindset and not want to take responsibility for your actions. This is where the growth begins, learning how to manoeuvre your life better. When I started to have a Growth mindset about life it helped me to understand when to have a certain mindset about something.

Now I can see things a lot clearer, and I always have a plan of action. This is where having a Fixed mindset helps with focus. For example, going to the gym three times a week. My approach to life was different. The Change mindset was now working for me. Altering my attitude gave me more opportunities. I found myself in better circles. Sometimes when life throws things at us and we don't know how to react. Mostly we act out of emotions not logic. Change only comes when you want it. Some things just must be left behind. Everything takes time to grow. Having a Growth mindset about life is like playing a game of chess. You must think two steps ahead. Be responsible. Stop blaming others for being the CEO of your life.

To improve is to change; to be perfect is to change often.
- Winston Churchill

DELICIOUS STIR FRY

History:

Courgettes, like all squash, have their ancestry in the Americas, specifically Mesoamerica. However, the varieties of green, cylindrical squash harvested immaturely and typically called "zucchini" were cultivated in northern Italy, as much as three centuries after the introduction of cucurbits from the Americas. It appears that this occurred in the second half of the 19th century, although the first description of the variety under the name zucchini occurs in a work published in Milan in 1901. Early varieties usually appended the names of nearby cities to their names.

Major Benefits:

Zucchini is also rich in antioxidants, contributes to healthy digestion, may reduce blood sugar levels, may improve heart health, may strengthen your vision, may aid weight loss, improve bone health, have anticancer effects, and encourage healthy prostate, and thyroid function.

Instructions:

Cook the egg noodles according to the package instructions, then drain and set aside.

In a wok or large frying pan, heat some vegetable oil over high heat.

Add the sliced mushrooms and sliced courgette to the wok and stir-fry for 2-3 minutes or until they are lightly browned and tender.

Add the sliced red chilli pepper, sliced green chilli pepper, and minced ginger to the wok and stir-fry for another minute or until fragrant.

Add the bean sprouts to the wok and stir-fry for 1-2 minutes or until they are lightly wilted.

Add the cooked egg noodles to the wok and stir-fry everything together for 1-2 minutes or until the noodles are heated through.

Pour the sweet chilli stir-fry sauce over the noodle mixture and stir everything together until well coated.

Add the chopped cashew nuts to the wok and stir-fry for another minute or until the cashews are lightly toasted.

Season with salt and black pepper to taste.

Serve hot and enjoy your delicious stir fry!

Fitness Session: 5

Game Changá mode

Target area: Whole-body workout

Warm-up then stretch for 10-15 minutes.

30 seconds for each exercise,
15 seconds rest,

Jumping jacks
Push-ups
Burpees
Sit-ups
Mountain climbers
Squats with a jump
Squat thrusts with a press-up

Finish off with warm-down and stretching exercises

Jumping jacks: Stand with your feet together and arms at your sides. Jump up, spreading your legs out to the sides and raising your arms above your head. Jump back to the starting position, bringing your feet together and lowering your arms to your sides. Repeat for 30 seconds. Rest for 15 seconds.

Push-ups: Start in a plank position with your hands slightly wider than shoulder-width apart. Lower your body until your chest nearly touches the floor, then push back up to the starting position. If you can't do a full push-up, you can modify it by doing them on your knees or against a wall. Repeat for 30 seconds. Rest for 15 seconds.

Burpees: Start in a standing position, then squat down and place your hands on the floor in front of you. Jump your feet back into a plank position, then immediately jump them back up towards your hands. Stand up and jump, reaching your arms above your head. Repeat for 30 seconds. Rest for 15 seconds.

Sit-ups: Lie on your back with your knees bent and feet flat on the floor. Place your hands behind your head or across your chest. Lift your upper body towards your knees, then lower back down. Repeat for 30 seconds. Rest for 15 seconds.

Mountain climbers: Start in a plank position with your hands directly under your shoulders. Bring one knee up towards your chest, then quickly switch and bring the other knee up. Repeat in a fast, alternating motion for 30 seconds. Rest for 15 seconds.

Squats with a jump: Stand with your feet shoulder-width apart. Lower your body down into a squat position, then explosively jump up, reaching your arms above your head. Land softly and immediately lower back down into a squat position. Repeat for 30 seconds. Rest for 15 seconds.

Squat thrusts with a press-up: Start in a standing position. Squat down and place your hands on the floor in front of you, then jump your feet back into a plank position. Do one push-up, then jump your feet back up towards your hands and stand up. Repeat for 30 seconds. Rest for 15 seconds.

After completing each exercise for 30 seconds, take a 15 second rest before moving on to the next exercise. Repeat the entire circuit twice, for a total of three rounds. Rest for 15 seconds.

To finish off the workout, do warm-down and stretching exercises for 10-15 minutes. Include gentle movements like walking or jogging, as well as stretches for all major muscle groups. Hold each stretch for 15-30 seconds, and remember to breathe deeply and relax.

Remember to stay hydrated throughout the workout and listen to your body. If you experience any pain or discomfort, stop the exercise and consult a healthcare professional.

Motivation: Do We Meet People For A Reason?

Every minute of the day we meet people. Going to school or college, our neighbours, on public transport or when we are travelling, in clubs, on holidays and the list goes on. We are all so caught up in our day-to-day lives that we miss opportunities and experiences we could have had, if only we had stopped for a minute and had a conversation. Remember, one second later or earlier and you have missed the person that you should have met.

People cross our paths for a reason and taking that one second to have a conversation could be the next game-changing power move that we were waiting for. When you put something out to the universe like a new dream job and you have no idea how you're going to get it. It could be that person who was sitting right beside you on the bus, tube, pub, or cafe was looking for a new employee, but you missed the opportunity. We all need good people in our lives and sometimes a stranger could be the missing link that we have been looking for.

See everyone as your next opportunity whether to help you or for you to help them. Make a sincere friend and enrich your life.

> **Each new friendship can make you a new person because it opens up new doors inside of you.**
>
> *- Kate DiCamillo*

GAME CHANGÁ PASTA

History

Kale originated in the eastern Mediterranean and Asia Minor, where it was cultivated for food beginning by 2000 BCE at the latest. Curly-leaved varieties of cabbage already existed along with flat-leaved varieties in Greece in the 4th century BC. These forms, which were referred to by the Romans as 'Sabellian Kale', are considered to be the ancestors of modern kales.

The earliest record of cabbages in western Europe is of hard-heading cabbage in the 13th century. Records in 14th-century England distinguish between hard-heading cabbage and loose-leaf kale. Russian kale was introduced into Canada, and then into the United States, by Russian traders in the 19th century.

Major Benefits:

Kale is loaded with powerful antioxidants like quercetin and kaempferol. It is an excellent source of vitamin C. Kale can help lower cholesterol, which may reduce the risk of heart disease. Kale is one of the world's best sources of vitamin K and beta-carotene, which are important nutrients. Kale is often claimed to be high in vitamin A, but this is not entirely accurate.

Instructions:

Cook the fusilli pasta according to the package instructions, then drain and set aside.

In a large frying pan, heat some olive oil over medium-high heat.

Add the sliced mushrooms to the pan and sauté for 2-3 minutes or until they are lightly browned and tender.

Add the chopped broccoli and kale to the pan and sauté for another 3-4 minutes or until the vegetables are tender.

Pour the coconut milk over the vegetables in the pan and stir everything together.

Add the chopped parsley to the pan and stir everything together again.

Reduce the heat to low and let the sauce simmer for 5-7 minutes or until it thickens slightly.

Season the sauce with salt and black pepper to taste.

Add the cooked fusilli pasta to the pan and toss everything together until the pasta is coated in the sauce.

Serve hot and enjoy your creamy and nutritious pasta dish!

Fitness Session: 6

Target area: Whole-body workout

Warm-up and Stretches:
10-15 minutes

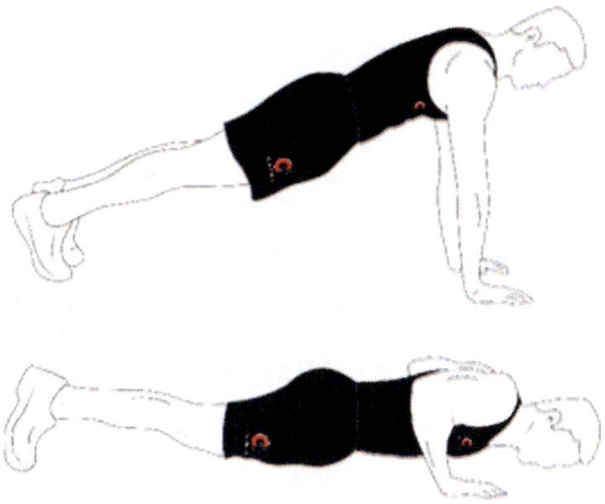

Push-ups: 30 seconds,
15 seconds rest
Squat thrusts: 30 seconds,
15 seconds rest
Burpees: 30 seconds,
15 seconds rest
Jumping jacks: 30 seconds,
15 seconds rest Mountain
climbers: 30 seconds, 15
seconds rest
V-shape plank: 30 seconds, 15 seconds, rest
Tuck jumps 30: seconds 15 seconds rest

Do each exercise 3 times before moving on to the next stage.

Warm-up: Begin with a light cardio exercise like jogging, jumping jacks or skipping rope for 5-10 minutes. Follow it up with some stretching exercises for the major muscle groups.

Push-ups: Start in a plank position with your hands placed shoulder-width apart on the floor. Lower your body until your chest touches the floor, then push yourself back up to the starting position. Repeat for 30 seconds, then rest for 15 seconds.

Squat thrusts: Start standing up, then squat down and place your hands on the floor in front of you. Jump your feet back to a plank position, then quickly jump them back up to your hands and stand up. Repeat for 30 seconds, then rest for 15 seconds.

Burpees: Start standing up, then squat down and place your hands on the floor in front of you. Jump your feet back to a plank position, then do a push-up. Jump your feet back up to your hands and jump up into the air, reaching your hands overhead. Repeat for 30 seconds, then rest for 15 seconds.

Jumping jacks: Stand up straight with your feet together and your arms by your sides. Jump your feet out to the sides and raise your arms overhead. Jump your feet back together and lower your arms to your sides. Repeat for 30 seconds, then rest for 15 seconds.

Mountain climbers: Start in a plank position with your hands shoulder-width apart on the floor. Bring one knee up to your chest, then quickly switch legs and bring the other knee up to your chest. Repeat as quickly as possible for 30 seconds, then rest for 15 seconds.

V-shape plank: Start in a plank position with your hands shoulder-width apart on the floor. Lift your hips up and back so that your body forms a V shape, then return to the starting position. Repeat for 30 seconds, then rest for 15 seconds.

Tuck jumps: Stand up straight, then jump up into the air and tuck your knees up to your chest. Land softly and immediately jump up again. Repeat for 30 seconds, then rest for 15 seconds.

Repeat each exercise for 3 sets before moving on to the next exercise. Remember to maintain good form throughout your workout.

When you have finished, walk or jog in place for a few minutes to lower your heart rate before stretching for 10-15 minutes to warm-down.

Good luck and have fun!

Remember to stay hydrated throughout the workout and listen to your body. If you experience any pain or discomfort, stop the exercise and consult a healthcare professional.

Motivation: Get To Know Yourself

With our busy lives of families, work, social media, and relationships we have no time for ourselves. Most of the decisions we make are because of the people around us. We need reassurance from people that sometimes don't have our best interests at hand. When is the last time you really decided something by yourself? Think about it. When you're going out you may ask a friend, "What do you think about this outfit?" When you go on holiday you ask, "Where we should go?" At all times we are searching for reassurance.

I ask myself from time to time, "How well do I know myself? " How many times have you heard people say, "You have changed." or "I never knew they could do that." At one time we knew what colour we liked, what food we wanted to eat, and what places we wanted to go to. But for some reason, we stop improving ourselves. Value yourself, then no matter what happens, learn to love you. And the only true way to start to live like this is to spend some time by yourself.

Take a walk by yourself, go on holiday by yourself, go on a night out by yourself. Find time to spend by yourself. The key is to get to know yourself. Find out what you really like, what makes you tick. Fall in love with yourself. Start looking within. That way you will start to find out things about yourself you didn't know. Make time for you. Turn off your phone, and your TV and give your mind time to wonder. Try to do this every day. Just that 10 minutes by yourself will start to make a big difference in your life, career, and relationships.

We understand how important it is to live in a good area. When we have children, we tend to look for good schools. This is all because we know the value of these things what we see and hear can affect us greatly. My environment has helped to shape me as I got older.

Growing up in Moss Side in the 1990s wasn't a place for a young child with no solid role model. There was too much for a young child to see. The drugs, needles, drug addicts, Police, abandoned houses, burnt-out motorcycles or cars, and schools that no one cared for. All these things contributed to how

I view the world over the years. As I got older my attitude changed. I knew that I had to be a certain way to not become a victim of the streets or my neighbourhood. Sometimes I ask myself, was the person I became really me or a product of my environment? If I was bought up in a completely different area with great role models would my mindset be the same? Would I have hobbies? Would the teachers in my school have my best interests in mind? With all these things going on in your head and all around you, at what point do you get to know yourself? Before you know it, a child comes along and now you must think about someone else.

Over the years I have had to reinvent myself and take on opportunities that I thought were beyond me. It has taken years to even find out what my interests and hobbies are. The colours that I like. The list goes on. Most of the time I was living my life through other people's eyes, not taking the time to find out what I want. I guess this is what we call growing up too quickly. I also grew up with a lot of girls and in some areas it was great. For instance, when I had my own children, I could do their hair.

The downside for me was I seemed to be very emotional all the time and did not know how to control it.

Once you give yourself the time to start to get to know yourself, the people around you start to change. The places you once to visited don't feel the same. You look at yourself in a different light and you probably won't recognise your old self. Why is it important to take time out for you? Because it gives you the time you may need to look inside yourself and see what it is that you really want from life. The opportunity to be the person that you should have been. The more I get to understand myself the more I love myself.

"
To grow yourself,
you must know
yourself.
- John C. Maxwell

THE HEALING DISH

History

Chickpeas, also known as garbanzo beans, have been grown and eaten in Middle Eastern countries for thousands of years. Their nutty taste and grainy texture pair well with many other foods and ingredients.

As a rich source of vitamins, minerals, and fibre, chickpeas may offer a variety of health benefits, such as aiding weight management, improving digestion, and reducing your risk of disease.

Additionally, this legume is high in protein and makes an excellent replacement for meat in many vegetarian and vegan dishes.

Major Benefits:

Chickpeas boast an impressive nutritional profile. They contain a moderate number of calories, providing 269 per cup (164 grams). Approximately 67% of these calories come from carbs, while the rest comes from protein and fat. Chickpeas also provide a variety of vitamins and minerals, as well as a decent amount of fibre and protein.

Instructions:

Rinse 200g quinoa in cold water, drain and transfer to a saucepan with 400ml of water. Bring to a boil, then reduce heat and let it simmer for 15-20 minutes, or until the quinoa is tender and the water has been absorbed.

While the quinoa is cooking, peel and dice 1 sweet potato into small cubes. Cut 1/2 yellow pepper and 1/2 red pepper into thin strips. Cut 6 okras into small pieces. Peel and finely chop 3 cloves of garlic.

Heat some oil in a large frying pan over medium-high heat. Add the sweet potato cubes and fry until lightly browned and almost cooked through, about 5-7 minutes.

Add the garlic, yellow pepper, red pepper, and okra to the pan. Cook for another 5-7 minutes, stirring occasionally until the vegetables are tender.

Drain and rinse 1 tin of chickpeas and add to the pan. Stir in 4 sprigs of thyme leaves (or 1 tsp of dried thyme) and season with salt and pepper to taste.

Once the quinoa is cooked, add it to the pan and stir everything together. Remove the pan from the heat and let it sit for a few minutes to let the flavours meld together.

Finely chop 3 sprigs of coriander and sprinkle over the top of the dish before serving. Enjoy!

Fitness Session: 7

Target area: Whole-body workout

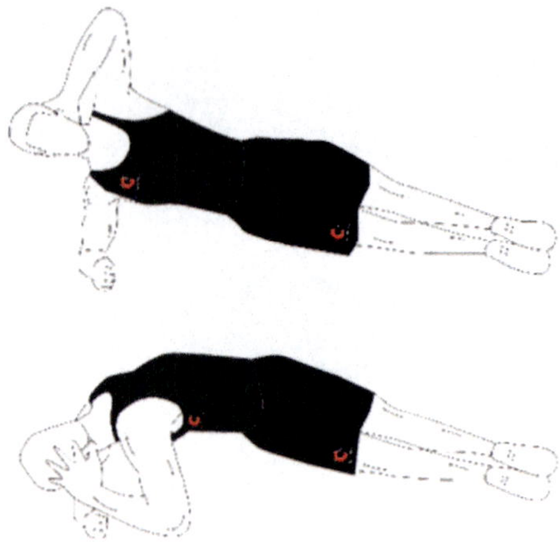

Warm-up then stretches for 10-15 minutes

Lunges (alternate legs):
30 seconds, 15 seconds rest
Push-ups (thumbs together):
30 seconds, 15 seconds rest
Sit-ups/crunches:
30 seconds, 15 seconds rest
Bear crawl (back and forth):
30 seconds, 15 seconds rest
Dips (thumbs touching):
30 seconds, 15 seconds rest
Star jumps: 30 seconds, 15 seconds rest
Skis: 30 seconds, 15 seconds rest
Each exercise 3 reps

Finish off with warm-down and stretching exercises.

Warm-up and Stretches: Start with some light cardio exercises such as jogging or jumping jacks for 5-10 minutes to get your heart rate up and your body warmed up. Perform static stretches for the major muscle groups such as hamstrings, quadriceps, calves, chest, back, and shoulders. Hold each stretch for 15-30 seconds and repeat 2-3 times.

Lunges: Stand with your feet shoulder-width apart and take a big step forward with your right leg, lowering your body until your right knee is at a 90-degree angle. Keep your left knee off the ground and your upper body straight. Push back up to the starting position and repeat with the left leg. Alternate legs for 30 seconds. Then rest for 15 seconds.

Push-ups with thumbs together: Start in a plank position with your hands shoulder-width apart and your thumbs touching. Lower your body until your chest touches the ground and then push back up to the starting position. Repeat for 30 seconds. Then rest for 15 seconds.

Sit-ups/Crunches: Lie on your back with your knees bent and your hands behind your head. Lift your upper body off the ground and crunch your abs, then lower back down to the starting position. Repeat for 30 seconds. Then rest for 15 seconds.

Bear Crawl: Start in a plank position with your hands and feet shoulder-width apart. Move forward by crawling on your hands and feet, keeping your body low to the ground. Then move backwards in the same manner. Repeat for 30 seconds. Then rest for 15 seconds.

Dips with thumbs touching: Sit on the edge of a bench or chair with your hands on the edge next to your hips, thumbs touching. Lower your body down by bending your elbows until your arms are at a 90-degree angle, then push back up to the starting position. Repeat for 30 seconds. Then rest for 15 seconds.

Star jumps: Stand with your feet shoulder-width apart and arms by your sides. Jump up and spread your legs and arms out to form a star shape in the air, then land back on the ground with your feet together and arms by your sides. Repeat for 30 seconds. Then rest for 15 seconds.

Skis: Stand with your feet together and jump side to side, keeping your feet together and your knees slightly bent. Land softly and quickly and use your arms to help with the momentum. Repeat for 30 seconds. Then rest for 15 seconds.

Warm-down: Perform some light cardio exercises such as jogging or walking for 5-10 minutes to cool down your body. Then perform some static stretches for the major muscle groups, holding each stretch for 15-30 seconds and repeating 2-3 times.

Remember to stay hydrated throughout the workout and listen to your body. If you experience any pain or discomfort, stop the exercise and consult a healthcare professional.

Motivation: Autopilot

What is the definition of autopilot? When we think about this, what comes to mind is being on a plane, ship, or train. Autopilot is a function to make our lives easier but is it really? Having autopilot on a plane allows the captain to undertake other tasks or take a break. In these circumstances, autopilot is a great thing. But to be on autopilot in life is not so.

From when you wake up until the time you leave the house. you have undertaken several tasks without thinking. For example, tidying your bed, brushing your teeth, taking a shower, using the toilet, and eating your breakfast. These are all tasks that you do every day without thinking. The real problem kicks in, is when we go through our whole day like this. If you could reverse your whole day from start to finish and do the same sequence for over a week, would there be any real change? Does your job challenge you? Do you take the same route every day? Then you come home and watch TV or go on social media sites more than you should. Does your life seem like Groundhog Day?

What being on autopilot means is that we all do things unconsciously for years and years and we never question them. I'm referring to the bad habits that we seem to have that never really benefit us. For the majority of my life, I have been living on autopilot. Let me just take a little time to give you an example of what autopilot is to me. Sometimes I found autopilot to be my best friend other times my worst enemy. Being able to deal with any situation that I came up against was always a good thing for me. Not letting my circumstances get me down for too long. Being able to bounce back. That part of my life was great.

But on the other side, I worked at jobs that I didn't like for longer than I should have. Every day was like Groundhog Day. This is not to say that you can't still excel. For me, my life was still going well, being able to hold a job for years and take care of my family. The thing was I did this without thinking; going to work, coming home, looking after the children. These are all things you can do without really trying. It doesn't take a lot to go through your day without really thinking. Most of the jobs that I have had did not take much brain power.

you just had to show up and follow orders. Then come home and continue the routine. I could honestly say that I could go through most days without a thought coming into my head. That's what autopilot meant to me; getting through your day with any real effort. I found myself just living with no goals, no plan, and no direction. Mostly living off hope.

I spent years of my life like this and still achieved a lot of success in many areas. Now I say to myself, imagine if I had a plan or learned to set goals how far would I be now in my life right now? Autopilot kept me in my safety zone, not burning out, always thinking safe. I realised that autopilot was working against me. Things needed to change. I began by setting goals for myself, having targets and holding myself responsible instead of living off hope. I can say this is where things started to come together for me real change. Being on autopilot can sometimes stunt our growth. But sometimes it is necessary. One of the key factors is to know when to turn on autopilot. Pilots normally engage the autopilot when the plane is cruising at a safe altitude and all the safety checks are done.

To change this concept in your life is to try something new every day. Go a different way to work? Try something different to eat. Have a day where you just mix it up and try new things. Do things that make you think. Do something that makes you scared. Get your blood pumping around the body. This is one of the ways to have new adventures and a fulfilling life.

> **The human spirit lives on creativity and dies in conformity and routine.**
>
> *- Vilayat Inayat Khan*

TROPICAL FLAVOURS

History

The cashew is native to Northeastern Brazil and Southeastern Venezuela and later was distributed around the world in the 1500s by Portuguese explorers. Portuguese colonists in Brazil began exporting cashew nuts as early as the 1550s. The Portuguese took it to Goa, India between 1560 and 1565. From there, it spread throughout Southeast Asia, and eventually Africa.

Major Benefits

Cashews are low in sugar and rich in fibre, heart-healthy fats, and plant protein. They're also a good source of copper, magnesium, and manganese — nutrients important for energy production, brain health, immunity, and bone health. Cashews are rich in a range of nutrients.

Instructions:

In a large frying pan, heat some olive oil over medium-high heat.

Add the sliced mushrooms and diced eggplant to the pan and sauté for 5-7 minutes or until the vegetables are tender and lightly browned.

Add the diced red pepper to the pan and sauté for another 2-3 minutes.

Add the chopped kale to the pan and stir everything together.

Season the mixture with salt and black pepper to taste.

Add the halved cherry tomatoes to the pan and stir everything together again.

Add the chopped spring onions and diced avocado to the pan and stir everything together.

Stir-fry for another 2-3 minutes or until the avocado is slightly softened.

Finally, add the handful of cashew nuts to the pan and stir everything together one last time.

Serve hot and enjoy your delicious and healthy tropical flavours!

Fitness Session: 8

Game Changá moment

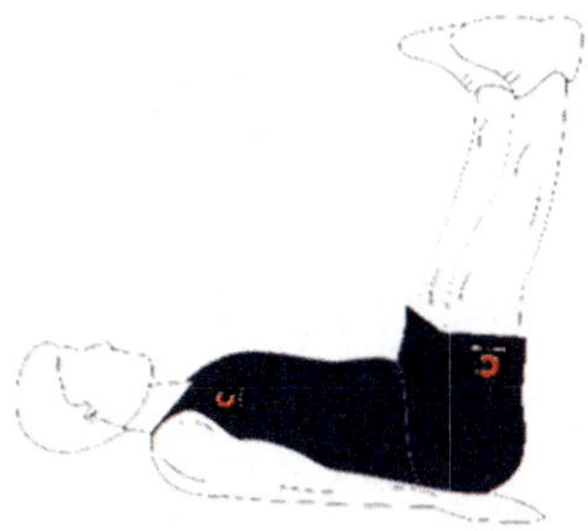

Target area: Whole-body workout

Warm-up then stretches for 10-15 minutes.

No rest. Do your best.

The pyramid sequence starts with one of each exercise:

1 Push-up
1 Burpee
1 Tuck jump
1 Walk-down push-up
1 Skip lunge
10 seconds Sprint on the spot

Then add on 1 rep to each exercise.

Your target is reps of 10, with no rest.
After finishing, warm-down and stretch.

Warm-up and Stretches: Start with light cardio exercises like jogging, jumping jacks, or skipping rope for 10-15 minutes to increase your heart rate and body temperature and increase blood flow to your muscles. Follow up your warm-up with dynamic stretches that target your major muscle groups, like leg swings, arm circles, and lunges. These stretches should prepare your muscles for the upcoming workout. Finish the warm-up with some light static stretches, holding each stretch for 10-15 seconds. Examples include hamstring stretches, quad stretches, and shoulder stretches.

This is a Pyramid sequence workout that involves increasing reps of different exercises with each round. Here's how to do it:

Round 1: Do 1 push-up, 1 burpee, 1 tuck jump, 1 walk-down push-up, 1 skip lunge, and 10 seconds of sprinting on the spot.

Start with 1 push-up: Begin in a plank position with your hands shoulder-width apart, core engaged, and back straight. Lower your body until your chest touches the floor, then push back up to the starting position. Repeat for one rep.

Add 1 burpee: From a standing position, jump up and land in a squat position with your hands on the ground. Kick your feet back to a plank position, perform a push-up, then jump your feet back to the squat position and stand up. Repeat for one rep.

Add 1 tuck jump: Start in a standing position, then jump as high as you can while bringing your knees up towards your chest. Land softly and repeat for one rep.

Add 1 walk-down push-up: Start in a standing position, then bend forward at the waist and walk your hands out until you're in a plank position. Walk your hands back towards your feet and stand up. Repeat for one rep.

Add 1 skip lunge: Start in a lunge position with your right foot forward, then jump up and switch your feet in mid-air so that your left foot is now forward. Repeat, alternating legs, for one rep.

Add 10 seconds of sprinting on the spot: Run on the spot as fast as you can for 10 seconds.

Repeat the entire sequence, adding one rep to each exercise each time through, until you reach your desired number of reps or time limit. Make sure to rest as needed and hydrate throughout the workout.

Round 2: Do 2 push-ups, 2 burpees, 2 tuck jumps, 2 walk-down push-ups, 2 skip lunges, and 10 seconds of sprinting on the spot.

Round 3: Do 3 push-ups, 3 burpees, 3 tuck jumps, 3 walk-down push-ups, 3 skip lunges, and 10 seconds of sprinting on the spot.

Round 4: Do 4 push-ups, 4 burpees, 4 tuck jumps, 4 walk-down push-ups, 4 skip lunges, and 10 seconds of sprinting on the spot.

Round 5: Do 5 push-ups, 5 burpees, 5 tuck jumps, 5 walk-down push-ups, 5 skip lunges, and 10 seconds of sprinting on the spot.

After completing Round 5, you can rest for a minute and repeat the entire sequence, aiming to complete 10 reps of each exercise in each round.

Warm-down: Finish your workout with static stretches that target the muscles you worked, like hamstring stretches, quad stretches, and shoulder stretches. These stretches will help your muscles recover and prevent soreness.

Remember to stay hydrated throughout the workout and listen to your body. If you experience any pain or discomfort, stop the exercise and consult a healthcare professional.

Motivation: The Importance Of A Role Model

For some of us, growing up in our household and finding a good role model was non-existent. We go through life making mistakes that we could have avoided with a good role model in our life. Most people around us haven't really achieved all that they could in life, limiting their potential and projecting the same limitations on us.

Having a mentor or a role model in your life is a particularly important part of growing up. Even the people that inspire us on TV and social media all have mentors or good role models in their lives. Most of us have a device in our hands. With a touch of a button, we can be exposed to inspirational, motivational people all around the world. We have no excuses. A friend of mine told me his father wasn't a good role model so he adopted Les Brown as his father. This gave him the motivation and inspiration he needed to move his life forwards. Every person has a great story to tell and each person had or has a role model.

Our first role models are our parents, relatives and close friends we look up to. I spent most of my childhood in Jamaica and came to England at the age of 9 years old. My mother at the time stayed back with my younger sister. There was no father figure all through my childhood. Even though I was living with family, the love of my own mother wasn't there. This led me to believe that I was not very welcome. We all know how children can be cruel at times and I had my fair share of living with my cousins. There was no one to run to when I seemed to have problems and no one to get advice from, so a lot of mistakes were made.

Even as a child, I could see the difference. How my cousins were because they had parents to run to for help and someone to look after them in their time of need. The only time you know that something is missing is when you see someone else with it. As time went on more mistakes were made. Every lesson seemed to be a hard lesson to learn. I am not too sure when I found someone to look up to, but change started happening around my late 20s. I think it was my gym crew. I was able to share ideas and be around people that were doing great things. They seemed to inspire me to look at my own life. I also started to read and listen to motivational speakers. I found my role model in the books and I started to set goals.

I remember when I bought my first house, I felt so proud of myself. It took me years down the line to understand how having great people in my life can help shape me in the right way. Now that I have my own children, I give them the guidance and advice that I lacked as a young child. And I can see the difference in their personalities in how they deal with problems. Having a great role model in your life is like having SAT-NAV; someone to guide you along the way and give you advice when needed including positive criticism.

“
Children have never been very good at listening to their elders, but they have never failed to imitate them.
- James Baldwin

HEALTHY QUINOA

History

Quinoa is an Andean plant that originated in the area surrounding Lake Titicaca in Peru and Bolivia. Quinoa was cultivated and used by pre-Columbian civilizations and was replaced by cereals on the arrival of the Spanish, despite being a local staple food at the time. Eaten for more than 5,000 years, quinoa continues to rise in popularity today thanks to its impressive nutritional profile. It comes in a variety of colours, each with subtle differences in flavour, texture, and nutrition.

Major Benefits

Quinoa is a good source of several important nutrients, including folate, magnesium, zinc, and iron. It is packed with nutrients, contains antioxidant and anti-inflammatory plant compounds, and is higher in fibre than many grains. It is gluten-free and great for people with gluten intolerance. It is high in important vitamins and minerals and is a good source of protein.

Instructions:

Rinse the quinoa in a fine mesh strainer and add it to a pot with 2 cups of water. Bring to a boil, then reduce the heat to low, cover, and simmer for 15-20 minutes, until the water is absorbed and the quinoa is tender.

While the quinoa is cooking, preheat the oven to 400°F (200°C) and line a baking sheet with parchment paper.

In a large bowl, combine the drained chickpeas, diced sweet potato, diced red pepper, diced yellow pepper, minced garlic, dried thyme, ground coriander, salt, and pepper. Toss to coat everything evenly.

Spread the vegetable mixture out in a single layer on the prepared baking sheet and roast for 20-25 minutes, until the sweet potato is tender and the vegetables are lightly browned.

While the vegetables are roasting, cook the sliced okra in a nonstick skillet over medium-high heat for 5-7 minutes, until lightly browned and tender.

When everything is done cooking, combine the quinoa, roasted vegetables, and cooked okra in a large bowl and toss to combine.

Serve warm and enjoy!

Fitness Session: 9

Target area: Whole-body workout

Warm-up then stretches for 10-15 minutes

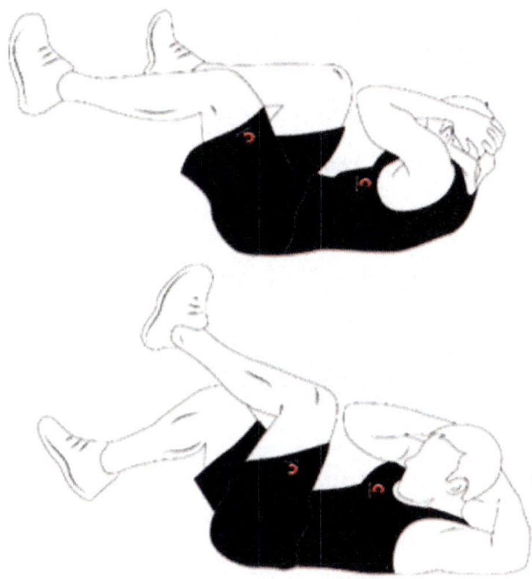

Mountain climbers:

30 seconds, 15 seconds rest

Tuck jumps: 30 seconds, 15 seconds rest

Walk-down push-ups:
30 seconds, 15 seconds rest

V-shape sit-ups:
30 seconds, 15 seconds rest

Up-down plank: 30 seconds, 15 seconds rest

Sprint on the spot: 30 seconds, 15 seconds rest

Jumping jacks: 30 seconds, 15 seconds rest

Dips (thumbs-touching): 30 seconds, 15 seconds rest

Push-up position, open and close legs: 30 seconds, 15 seconds rest

Lunges: 30 seconds, 15 seconds rest

Warm-down and Stretching.

Warm-up and Stretches: Begin with warm-up exercises and stretches to get your body ready for the workout. Start with a light jog or march in place for a few minutes to get your heart rate up and loosen up your muscles.

Mountain climbers: Get into a plank position with your arms straight and your hands directly under your shoulders. Bring your right knee towards your chest, then return to the starting position and repeat with your left leg. Alternate between your right and left legs for 30 seconds. Then rest for 15 seconds.

Tuck jumps: Stand with your feet shoulder-width apart, then jump up and bring your knees up to your chest. Land softly and repeat for 30 seconds. Then rest for 15 seconds.

Walk-down push-ups: Stand with your feet shoulder-width apart, then bend forward and place your hands on the floor. Walk your hands out into a plank position, perform a push-up, then walk your hands back towards your feet and stand up. Repeat for 30 seconds. Then rest for 15 seconds.

V-shape sit-ups: Lie on your back with your legs straight and your arms extended above your head. Lift your legs and torso off the ground at the same time and touch your hands to your feet. Lower yourself back down and repeat for 30 seconds. Then rest for 15 seconds.

Up-down plank: Get into a plank position with your arms straight and your hands directly under your shoulders. Lower yourself down onto your forearms one arm at a time, then push yourself back up onto your hands one arm at a time. Repeat for 30 seconds. Then rest for 15 seconds.

Sprint on the spot: Run in place as fast as you can for 30 seconds. Then rest for 15 seconds.

Jumping jacks: Stand with your feet together and your arms at your sides. Jump up and spread your legs out to the sides while raising your arms above your head. Jump back to the starting position and repeat for 30 seconds. Then rest for 15 seconds.

Dips (thumbs-touching): Sit on the edge of a chair or bench with your hands on the edge and your fingers pointing forward. Lower yourself down by bending your arms, and keeping your elbows close to your sides. Push yourself back up and touch your thumbs together at the top. Repeat for 30 seconds. Then rest for 15 seconds.

Push-up position, open and close legs: Get into a push-up position with your arms straight and your hands directly under your shoulders. Open your legs out to the sides, then bring them back together. Repeat for 30 seconds. Then rest for 15 seconds.

Lunges: Stand with your feet hip-width apart, then take a big step forward with your right foot and lower your body until your right knee is bent at a 90-degree angle. Push back up to the starting position and repeat with your left leg. Alternate between your right and left legs for 30 seconds. Then rest for 15 seconds.

Warm-down and Stretches: Once you've completed all the exercises, cool down with some light stretches to help your muscles relax and prevent injury. Stretch your arms, legs, and core, holding each stretch for 20-30 seconds.

Remember to stay hydrated throughout the workout and listen to your body. If you experience any pain or discomfort, stop the exercise and consult a healthcare professional.

Motivation: Growth Is On The Other Side

The human brain is a remarkable organ that is designed to keep us safe. It instinctively reacts to anything that deviates from the norm with a fight-or-flight response. However, there is a fine line between being ordinary and achieving greatness. We often talk ourselves out of pursuing our dreams because we fear the unknown. But deep down, we all desire to live a fulfilling life.

We are all unique in our own way. But in order to truly unlock our full potential, we must embark on a journey of self-development. This journey is never-ending and requires consistent effort and dedication. It's like an athlete who, upon finishing one race, immediately begins preparing for the next one. The key is to enjoy the journey, embracing who we are becoming along the way. As long as we are moving forward towards our goals, we will continue to grow and evolve.

> A dream doesn't become a reality through magic; it takes sweat, determination, and hard work.
>
> *- Colin Powell*

PUMPKIN MASALA

History

Pumpkins, like other squash, originated in northeastern Mexico and the southern United States. The oldest evidence is pumpkin fragments found in Mexico that are dated between 7,000 and 5,500 BC. Pumpkin fruits are a type of botanical berry known as pepo.

Major Benefits

Pumpkin is a good source of vitamins and minerals like vitamin A, vitamin B2, vitamin C, vitamin E, iron, copper, manganese, and potassium. It is highly nutritious and particularly rich in Vitamin A, high in antioxidant content, and may reduce your risk of chronic diseases. Pumpkin packs vitamins that may boost immunity, lutein, and zeaxanthin that may protect your eyesight, and its nutrient density and low-calorie count may promote weight loss.

Instructions:

Preheat the oven to 200°C (400°F).

Rinse the rice with cold water until the water runs clear. Then, place it in a pot with 2 cups of water and a pinch of salt. Bring the water to a boil, then reduce the heat to low, cover the pot with a lid, and simmer for 10-12 minutes, or until the rice is cooked through.

While the rice is cooking, prepare the vegetables. Peel and chop the carrot into small pieces. Cut the eggplant, pumpkin, and courgette into bite-sized cubes. Finely chop the onion.

Heat a large pan over medium-high heat. Once hot, add a small amount of oil and swirl it around to coat the pan. Add the chopped vegetables to the pan and sauté for 5-7 minutes, or until they are slightly softened and browned.

Add the Saag Masala sauce to the pan with the vegetables and stir well to combine. Reduce the heat to low, cover the pan with a lid, and let the sauce simmer for 5-7 minutes, or until the vegetables are fully cooked and the sauce has thickened.

Once the rice is cooked, fluff it with a fork and divide it evenly between two plates. Spoon the Saag Masala sauce and vegetables over the rice, and garnish with the spinach leaves.

Serve hot and enjoy!

Fitness Session: 10

Target area: Whole-body workout

Warm-up then stretches

1st set:

15 Burpees, 10 seconds Sprints on the spot, 10 seconds Lunges, 10 seconds Burpees

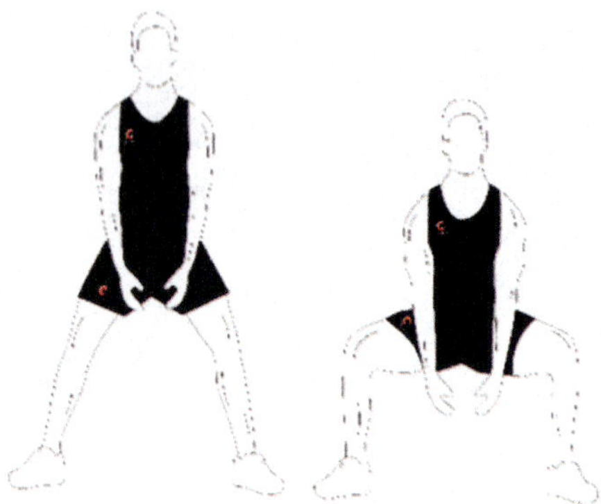

2nd set:

20 Jumping jacks, 10 seconds High knees, 10 seconds Squats, 10 seconds Jump squats.

3rd set:

15 Walk-down push-ups, 10 seconds Sprint on the spot, 10 seconds Lunges, 10 seconds Burpees.

4th set:

15 Mountain climbers, 10 seconds Sprint on the spot, 10 seconds Lunges,10 seconds Burpees.

Do your best. Rest for 15-30 seconds between sets. Finish with warm-down and stretching exercises.

Warm-up and Stretches: Start with light cardio exercises such as jogging or jumping jacks for 5-10 minutes to get your heart rate up and blood flowing. After the cardio, do some dynamic stretching exercises to warm up your muscles. Examples include arm circles, leg swings, and hip rotations.

Set 1: Start with 15 burpees. Begin in a standing position, squat down and place your hands on the ground, jump your feet back into a plank position, do a push-up, jump your feet back to your hands, and then jump up in the air with your arms overhead.

Immediately follow with 10 seconds of sprints on the spot. Run in place as fast as you can.

Next, do 10 seconds of lunges. Step forward with one foot, bend both knees, and lower your back knee toward the ground. Then, alternate legs.

Finish with 10 seconds of burpees.

Set 2: Start with 20 jumping jacks. Jump your feet out to the side and raise your arms overhead. Then, jump your feet back together and lower your arms.

Immediately follow with 10 seconds of high knees. Run in place and lift your knees up as high as you can.

Next, do 10 seconds of squats. Stand with your feet shoulder-width apart, bend your knees, and lower your hips down as if you are sitting in a chair.

Finish with 10 seconds of jump squats. From the squat position, jump up in the air and land back in the squat position.

Set 3: Start with 15 walk-down push-ups. Begin in a standing position, reach down and walk your hands out into a plank position, do a push-up, then walk your hands back up to standing.

Immediately follow with 10 second sprints on the spot. Run in place as fast as you can.

Next, do 10 seconds of lunges.

Finish with 10 seconds of burpees.

Set 4: Start with 15 mountain climbers. Begin in a plank position, bring your right knee up to your chest, then switch and bring your left knee up to your chest. Continue alternating.

Immediately follow with 10 second sprints on the spot. Run in place as fast as you can.

Next, do 10 seconds of lunges.

Finish with 10 seconds of burpees.

Warm-down and Stretches: After completing the sets, slow down your heart rate and stretch your muscles to prevent injury. Do static stretches such as hamstring stretches, quad stretches, and calf stretches, holding each stretch for 15-30 seconds. Finish with deep breathing exercises to calm your body and mind.

Remember to stay hydrated throughout the workout and listen to your body. If you experience any pain or discomfort, stop the exercise and consult a healthcare professional.

Motivation: 5 Second Rule

Do you find that you are always putting things off and never seem to get around to doing them? One of the main reasons for this is our brains don't like to do things that scare us or take us out of our comfort zone. How many times have you wanted to do something, but you find yourself doing other things instead? Then you see someone else doing it or one of your friends starts telling you how good they feel because they kept on doing it and you back out.

If I could have a penny for every time, I wished I had applied the 5 second rule, I would be rich already. What is the 5 second rule? Let me put it this way; how many times have you overreacted to something that didn't really mean anything? It was more of an emotional reaction. I have had a few encounters where something was happening and by the time I reached home, I wasn't happy with the outcome. One of those moments when you're not happy with yourself and the situation keeps going over and over in your head. By giving yourself time to think before you react, you may get a completely different outcome.

Every time I reflect on my childhood and becoming a young man, most of my life decisions were made by an emotional reaction and they were not the best choices. I didn't know to think before I opened my mouth. I never thought about the consequences. It was mainly, take it as it comes. It was as if I didn't have a sense of living, never caring about my actions. I guess I had a hate for the world and everyone in it. What you put out is what you get back and all I was pushing out was negativity and bad energy. Until I truly understood, that I was my own worst enemy, I just kept on blaming the world for my problems. I didn't even consider that it was my attitude towards life.

Maya Angelou said, "Do the best you can until you know better. Then when you know better, do better." I had very poor role models and it was only when I stopped making excuses for my actions and wanted better for myself. This was hard to take in when you have grown up to see kindness as a weakness. It was about winning and losing when a situation made me feel uncomfortable. By this, I'm talking about my ego and pride that I allowed to get in my way and cause me to react unproductively towards that situation. But once I could see the problem for what it was I made the effort to fix it.

There is an old saying by Tao Te Ching; "When the student is ready the teacher will appear." My teachers were the inspirational speakers and books that I started to buy. Every time I heard something that made me think I tried to apply it throughout the day. This is where the 5 second rule came in. On my journey to improving myself, I would come across many things that would make me pause and count down from 5 to 1 before I gave myself a push and adapted. Let's say that I'm driving and someone cuts me off. Before I would have reacted with road rage. But now I found myself thinking differently. Things like; "Maybe they're in a rush because they're late or something must have happened." It was no longer about my ego or pride. Just like anything else it takes practice. There were times I got caught off guard and went back to my old ways. But the difference was I could now identify that the problem and solution lie in how I react. I knew about it and I could see it working. The smallest things can upset our day even down to a phone call if we let it. Try this the next time the phone rings and you know that the person on the other side may upset you. You let the phone ring for a few seconds before you pick it up and give yourself those 5 seconds.

When you have something that you want to achieve, try counting down 5,4,3,2,1 and just do it. If you're in your bed and you want to start training, as soon as the alarm clock goes off, count 5,4,3,2,1 and then just get out of bed and start. Don't press the snooze button. If there is something you have been putting off, do your countdown 5,4,3,2,1 and get it done. Repetition is key. Try it right now. Remember there is no growth in the comfort zone, just the same results that you have been getting over the years. If you want to change, it starts with you.

> Don't put off till tomorrow what you can do today.
>
> *- Benjamin Franklin*

ASPARAGUS, BUTTER BEANS AND SWEET POTAT

History

The history of asparagus goes back as far as that of the leek and has been consumed for over 2000 years. This garden plant originated in the eastern Mediterranean countries and traces of wild varieties have been discovered in Africa. Archaeologists believe that it was also cultivated in Egypt.

Major Benefits

It's low in calories and a great source of nutrients, including fibre, folate, and vitamins A, C, and K. Additionally, eating asparagus has several potential health benefits, including weight loss, improved digestion, healthy pregnancy outcomes, and lower blood pressure. Thanks to their diuretic function, they help the cleansing process by activating the functions of the liver and kidneys that eliminate the toxins. It is low in calories and a great source of nutrients, including fibre, folate is also known as vitamin b9, and vitamins A, C, and K. Asparagus can help you lose weight, and is easy to add to your diet. It is a good source of antioxidants which are compounds that help protect your cells from the harmful effects of free radicals and oxidative stress.

Instructions:

Preheat your oven to 200°C (400°F).

In a large mixing bowl, toss the diced sweet potato with some olive oil and a pinch of salt and black pepper.

Spread the sweet potato pieces out on a baking tray and roast them in the preheated oven for 15-20 minutes, or until tender and lightly browned.

In the meantime, heat some olive oil in a large frying pan over medium-high heat.

Add the sliced mushrooms to the pan and sauté for 3-5 minutes, or until lightly browned.

Add the chopped asparagus and diced courgette to the pan and stir everything together.

Season the mixture with salt and black pepper to taste.

Add the diced tomato to the pan and stir everything together again.

Finally, add the butter beans to the pan and stir everything together

Fitness Session: 11

Target area: Arms, shoulders and upper back.

Tricep dips are a great exercise to strengthen and tone the muscles in the back of your arms. Here's how to do them:

Begin with warm-up and stretches for legs, hips, arms, shoulders and back.

Sit on the edge of a sturdy chair, a bench, or a step, with your hands gripping the front edge of the seat beside your hips. Your fingers should be pointing forward.

Slide your hips forward off the chair, supporting your weight with your arms. Your legs should be extended in front of you, with your feet flat on the ground.

Keeping your elbows close to your body, lower your body down by bending your elbows, until your arms form a 90-degree angle.

Push yourself back up to the starting position by straightening your elbows, without locking them.

Repeat for the desired number of reps.

End with warm-down and stretching exercises.

Tips For Proper Form:

Keep your shoulders down and away from your ears.

Keep your elbows close to your body to target the triceps.

Avoid letting your hips drop below the level of the seat, as this can strain your shoulders and wrists.

You can make this exercise easier by bending your knees and bringing your feet closer to the chair, or harder by straightening your legs and elevating your feet on another chair or step.

Remember to stay hydrated throughout the workout and listen to your body. If you experience any pain or discomfort, stop the exercise and consult a healthcare professional.

Motivation: Visualise, Believe, Time

Visualisation is a powerful tool to manifest your dreams and desires. It involves creating a mental image of what you want to achieve or experience. I call this the magic formula of being a child. As children we make-believe. We imagine that we are kings and queens, pirates of a ship, racecar drivers, or superheroes. At some stage in our lives, we stop believing so we also stop visualizing and lose the concept of time. Living in a pushbutton world with most things at our fingertips, makes us forget about time. We want things today. We no longer act out our dreams and our beliefs aren't as strong as they were.

Being able to visualize your goal is a very important and powerful tool. Let's take the example of an architect and a person that believes in faith. Both people can look at a piece of land and see things a normal eye cannot see. That is the power of visualization. See yourself two years from now and live like you are already there.

The process of creating a vision board helps you visualise what you want, and believe in your ability to achieve it. It is a way to tap into your creative potential and connect with your inner child's playful and imaginative nature. When you have a clear vision of what you want and believe in your ability to make it happen, you are more likely to take action and stay committed to your goals, even when the going gets tough.

The power of a vision board makes you remember what it was like to be a child all over again. Visualize, believe, and with time, anything is possible. The key is not to worry about reaching the finishing line but to get started. Just focus on getting one foot in front of the other and enjoy the journey.

The way to make your dreams come true is to start believing in them.
-Helen Barry

MIXED BEANS SALAD

History

Beans from their origins as a wild vine in Central and South America to the thousands of varieties grown around the world today have evolved to be one of the world's most important and versatile crops. The common bean (Phaseolus vulgaris) originated as a wild vine in Central and South America. Evidence also exists that suggests that native people of Mexico and Peru were cultivating bean crops as far back as 7000 BC. The use of lentils has been traced back as far as 6750 BC in parts of the present-day Middle East.

Major Benefits

Beans provide protein, fibre, folate, iron, potassium, and magnesium while containing little or no total fat, trans-fat, sodium, and cholesterol. Beans are high in amino acids, the building blocks of protein and an important source of plant-based protein so are a suitable replacement for meat in the diet. Those under age 65 require about 0.36 grams of protein per pound of body weight (0.8 grams per kilogram) — that's about 58 grams of protein for a person who weighs 160 pounds (72 kg). Beans contain several vital nutrients, including folate and antioxidants. They promote heart health and help to reduce the risk of cancer, and diabetes, promote glucose metabolism, prevent fatty liver, and control appetite.

Instructions:

Heat a large wok or frying pan over medium-high heat.

Add a splash of oil (such as vegetable or olive oil) and swirl to coat the pan.

Add the sliced spring onions and minced garlic to the pan and stir-fry for 1-2 minutes, until fragrant.

Add the asparagus pieces and sliced peppers to the pan and stir-fry for 3-4 minutes, until the vegetables are crisp-tender.

Add the sliced mushrooms to the pan and stir-fry for another 1-2 minutes, until the mushrooms are softened and lightly browned.

Add the halved cherry tomatoes and the drained and rinsed mixed beans to the pan and stir-fry for 2-3 minutes, until the tomatoes are slightly softened and the beans are heated through.

Season with salt and pepper to taste, and serve hot.

Enjoy your healthy and flavorful mixed bean and vegetable stir-fry!

Fitness Session: 12

Target area: Hips, legs

Squat jumps are a great exercise for improving lower body strength, explosive power, and overall fitness.

Here's a step-by-step guide on how to perform squat jumps:

Begin with some warm-up and stretching exercises for your legs.

Stand with your feet shoulder-width apart and toes pointing forward.

Squat down by pushing your hips back and bending your knees until your thighs are parallel to the ground. Keep your chest up and your core tight.

From the bottom of the squat position, push through your feet and jump up as high as you can, extending your arms overhead.

Land softly on the balls of your feet and immediately go back into the squat position, absorbing the impact with your legs.

Repeat the movement for the desired number of reps.

End with warm-down and stretching exercises.

Tips For Proper Form:

Keep your knees in line with your toes as you squat down and jump up.

Land softly to reduce the impact on your joints.

Keep your core tight throughout the movement to protect your lower back.

Aim for a full extension at the top of the jump by fully extending your hips and knees.

Start with a low number of reps and gradually increase as you get stronger and more comfortable with the movement.

Remember to always consult with a qualified fitness professional before starting any new exercise program, especially if you have any injuries or health concerns.

Remember to stay hydrated throughout the workout and listen to your body. If you experience any pain or discomfort, stop the exercise and consult a healthcare professional.

Motivation: Emotions

Think about this; out of ten situations you face daily, how many times is your answer out of logic and not emotions? We are all emotional people and some of us grow up with just our mothers and no fathers. Without a balance of both parents, if this is you, then like me we can adopt our mother's feminine side. When is the last time you really thought to yourself? "That person is right about what they are saying about me." Most of us will never admit to our wrongs or confess to our mistakes. We are quick to feel sorry for ourselves when there is no reason to.

I'm going to say, the world has gone soft. Kids are not allowed to play like children anymore, which can make them scared of every little thing when they get older. Emotions can cause us to make the wrong decisions. Emotions can keep you in a relationship that you know is not right for you, yet you stay. Emotions can have you living a life that is beneath you and not inspiring or motivating you. Let's get in control of our emotions and start to look at things logically.

Think about this; from the time you woke up this morning, how many different feelings have you had? There is a quote by Epictetus that says, "Any person capable of angering you becomes your master." This can be a hard pill to swallow. The subconscious mind can pick up things along the way without you even knowing it. Ask yourself, why do you get angry, sad, or frustrated? On the wheel of emotions, there are 34,000 emotions that you can go through.

As far as I remember back the only emotions that I really felt were sadness, happiness and anger. Mostly anger if I'm being totally honest with myself. As a child, I tended to look around at other people and wished that I had the same life as them. Which led to feeling down all the time. Kind of like always having a black raincloud over my head. Always expecting the worst from life. You have to understand that a big part of my childhood was spent in Jamaica it was only when I came here to the UK, my life seemed upside down. Which I guess made me angry. I wanted to go back.

Now when you practise something for a very long time it becomes a habit. It got to the point where all I felt most days was anger towards people, the environment, school my life. Everything was through my eyes and my eyes only. I didn't understand that when my mum was here in England my younger sister was in Jamaica basically by herself. And that's the reason why she couldn't stay for more than a year. That used to affect me deeply.

Anger affects your whole attitude and for me, my face couldn't hide how I was feeling. I think if you would have said Boo! to me, that would have gotten me angry. I also wanted my anger to last for as long as possible. I guess that way I could switch off completely. Go into myself thinking that I was winning, not understanding that I was losing the battle of life. This also habit followed me into adulthood.

My subconscious mind made it a blueprint without me knowing. at the time I even had this mindset toward my wife. When she got me angry I figured, I don't have to talk to her about it. It's like I wanted to make it hard for her. Kind of teach her a lesson not to get me angry. It seemed impossible to shake off, it was automatic and once it started I couldn't stop it. Now that would have probably been okay if it was just me and her. But we had children by then and things needed taking care of.

About 10 years ago we visited a friend from Egypt and I was telling him what I didn't like about myself. His response was when he and his wife argue, they dealt with it before going to bed. They never let it roll over into the next day. We both came home and put it into action. We still had our moments but now I had more tools to work with. Not understanding your emotions and why you are feeling that way can have an impact on your life and your well-being. Find the time to reflect and ask yourself, why am I feeling this way?

“

Attitude is everything, so pick a good one.

- Dr Wayne Dyer

MORNING WAKE UP

History

Blackberries are native to Asia, Europe, North America, Australia, Africa, and South America and have the most widespread geographic origin of any fruit crop. Later it was cultivated throughout the world with climates that support it. It has been used in Europe for 2000 years and is consumed as food, used for different medicinal purposes, and was grown in hedges to keep out invaders.

Major Benefits:

Blackberries offer many health benefits. They are high in fibre and may boost brain health. Apart from its wonderful and sweet taste, Blackberry is a good source of nutrients, minerals, and vitamins C and K.

Ingredients:

Assorted fruits of your choice (Apple, pomegranate and blackberries.)

1 tablespoon of honey or agave syrup (optional)

1 tablespoon of freshly squeezed lemon or lime juice (optional)

Mint leaves (optional)

Instructions:

Wash and cut all the fruits into bite-size pieces.

Add the cut fruits into a large mixing bowl.

If you prefer your fruit salad sweeter, drizzle honey or agave syrup over the fruits and gently toss to coat.

If you want your fruit salad to have a tangy flavour, squeeze a tablespoon of lemon or lime juice over the fruits and toss.

If you want to add some extra freshness, tear some mint leaves and sprinkle them over the fruit salad.

Gently toss all the ingredients together until the fruits are evenly coated.

Refrigerate the fruit salad for at least 30 minutes before serving.

Serve the fruit salad chilled and enjoy!

Note: You can customize your fruit salad by adding different fruits or adjusting the amount of sweet

Fitness Session: 13

Target area: Whole-body workout

Warm-up then stretches.

25-50 Crunches, twice

20 Jumping jacks

25-50 Burpees, twice

20 Jumping jacks

25-50 Push-ups, twice

20 Jumping jacks

60 Mountain climbers, twice

20 Jumping jacks

25 Squats with a jump

25 Normal squats

20 Jumping jacks

40 V-shape plank

20 Jumping jacks

25 Walk-out push-ups

20 Jumping jacks

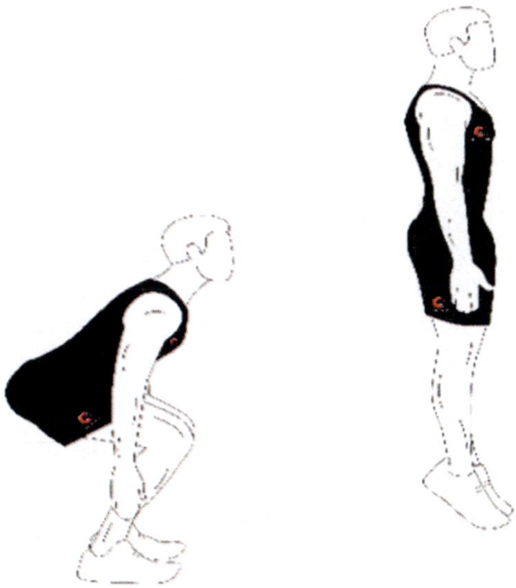

Each exercise is followed by 20 Jumping jacks. Do this circuit twice then warm-down and stretch.

Warm-up and Stretches: Start with some light cardio such as jogging in place or jumping jacks for 5-10 minutes to get your heart rate up and loosen up your muscles. After warming up, do some stretches for your major muscle groups such as hamstrings, quads, calves, back, shoulders, and neck. Hold each stretch for 15-30 seconds.

Crunches: Lie on your back with your knees bent and feet flat on the ground. Place your hands behind your head and lift your head, neck, and shoulders off the ground using your abdominal muscles. Lower back down and repeat for 25 to 50 reps, rest for 15 seconds and repeat.

Jumping jacks: Stand with your feet together and arms at your sides. Jump your feet out to shoulder-width apart while raising your arms overhead. Jump back to starting position and repeat for 20 reps. Rest for 15 seconds

Burpees: Start in a standing position, then squat down and place your hands on the ground in front of you. Jump your feet back into a plank position, then do a push-up. Jump your feet back up to your hands, stand up, and jump straight up. Repeat for 25 to 50 reps, rest for 15 seconds and repeat.

20 Jumping jacks

Push-ups: Start in a plank position with your hands slightly wider than shoulder-width apart. Lower your body down towards the ground by bending your elbows, then push back up to starting position. Repeat for 25 to 50 reps, rest for 15 seconds and repeat.

20 Jumping jacks

Mountain climbers: Start in a plank position with your hands directly under your shoulders. Bring one knee towards your chest, then quickly switch legs so the other knee comes towards your chest. Keep alternating legs as quickly as possible for 60 reps, rest for 15 seconds and repeat.

20 Jumping jacks

Squats with a jump: Start with your feet shoulder-width apart, squat down as if you're sitting in a chair, and then jump straight up. Land softly and repeat for 25 reps, then do 25 normal squats without the jump. Rest for 15 seconds and repeat.

Normal squats: Stand with your feet shoulder-width apart and toes pointing forward. Squat down by pushing your hips back and bending your knees until your thighs are parallel to the ground. Keep your chest up and your core tight. Slowly return to starting position.

20 Jumping jacks

V-shape plank: Start in a plank position with your feet wider than hip-width apart. Lift your left hand and right foot off the ground and hold for a few seconds, then switch sides. Repeat for 40 reps, rest for 15 seconds and repeat.

20 Jumping jacks

Walk-out push-ups: Stand up straight, then bend over and touch your toes. Walk your hands out until you are in a plank position, then do a push-up. Walk your hands back towards your feet and stand up straight. Repeat for 25 reps, rest for 15 seconds and repeat.

20 Jumping jacks

Finish off the workout with a warm-down and stretch for 10-15 minutes. This can include gentle movements like walking or jogging, as well as stretches for all major muscle groups. Hold each stretch for 15-30 seconds, and don't forget to breathe deeply and relax.

Remember to stay hydrated throughout the workout and listen to your body. If you experience any pain or discomfort, stop the exercise and consult a healthcare professional.

Motivation: Feelings Create Meaning

Motivation is a critical factor that drives us to achieve our goals and aspirations. However, often, we find ourselves struggling to accomplish the things we desire while accomplishing other things with ease. One of the reasons for this is the emotional attachment we have to the task at hand.

Everything we do has an emotional connection, and to accomplish something significant, we must venture into uncharted territories, which can trigger a range of emotions. If we lack the emotional drive to push through these emotions, we may find ourselves struggling to achieve our goals.

Whether it's losing weight, ending a relationship, or pursuing a dream job, the key to success lies in the strength of the emotions we attach to our actions. We often believe that we need external motivation, but the truth is that we convince ourselves that our desires do not matter enough.

The next time you find yourself struggling to step out of your comfort zone and pursue something significant, take a moment to reflect on your emotions. Ask yourself, what feelings am I experiencing? What emotions are holding me back, and how can I tap into the emotions that will drive me forward? By understanding and harnessing the power of our emotions, we can achieve anything we desire.

“

Let today be the day where you rise above the excuses.

-Hiral Nagda

SUNSHINE WAKE UP

History

Kiwi or Chinese gooseberry has a history of several thousand years. This plant is native to mainland China and Taiwan and grown commercially in New Zealand and California. This fruit has a slightly acidic taste and can be eaten raw or cooked. This juice is sometimes used as a meat softener. Raw kiwi is rich in vitamins C and K.

It was in the early 20th century that a missionary named Isabel Frazier brought the fruit from China to New Zealand after visiting schools in China. In 1906, the first kiwi tree was planted by a kindergartener named Alexander Allison, and by 1910 the first kiwi fruit was harvested in New Zealand. More and more growers started growing kiwifruit from Auckland, Wangwei, Fielding, and Tauranga. This fresh and juicy fruit was not called kiwi until 1958 when a fruit packing company in Auckland changed its name.

Major Benefits

The main properties of Kiwi are vitamins, minerals, proteins, and carbohydrates. The zero fat content of any kind makes this fruit so highly regarded by physicians and nutritionists. The vitamins it contains are vitamins A, B6, and B12, vitamin C, and D. The minerals contained in the fruit are sodium, potassium, calcium, iron, and magnesium. Foods rich in vitamins (A, B, C, D, E, and K) promote intestinal transit, it is an antioxidant food, with diuretic properties, Kiwi strengthens the immune system, and helps to prevent cardiovascular diseases.

Fruit salad is a refreshing and healthy dish that is easy to make. Here is a simple recipe to make a delicious fruit salad:

Ingredients:

Assorted fruits of your choice (strawberries, orange, pineapple, kiwi.)

1 tablespoon of honey or agave syrup (optional)

1 tablespoon of freshly squeezed lemon or lime juice (optional) Mint leaves (optional)

Instructions:

Wash and cut all the fruits into bite-size pieces.

Add the cut fruits into a large mixing bowl.

If you prefer your fruit salad sweeter, drizzle honey or agave syrup over the fruits and gently toss to coat.

If you want your fruit salad to have a tangy flavour, squeeze a tablespoon of lemon or lime juice over the fruits and toss.

If you want to add some extra freshness, tear some mint leaves and sprinkle them over the fruit salad.

Gently toss all the ingredients together until the fruits are evenly coated.

Refrigerate the fruit salad for at least 30 minutes before serving.

Serve the fruit salad chilled and enjoy!

Note: You can customize your fruit salad by adding different fruits or adjusting the amount of sweet

Fitness Session: 14

Target area: Whole-body workout

Warm-up then stretches

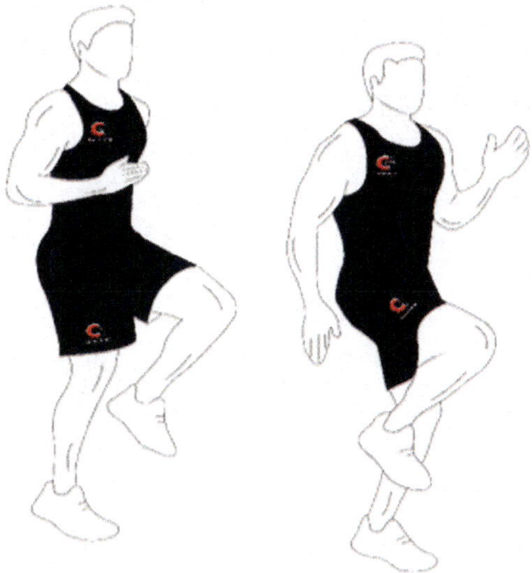

V-shape push-ups: 20

Sit-ups: 40

Shoulder taps: 20

Sit-ups: 40

Diamond-shaped push-ups: 20

Sit-ups: 40

Walk-out push-ups: 20

Sit-ups: 40

Wide-hand push-ups: 20

Sit-ups: 40

Squat thrust push-ups: 20

Sit-ups: 40

Mountain climbers: 30 seconds

Sit-ups: 40

Star jumps: 20

Sit-ups: 40

Bear crawl: 30 seconds

Sit-ups: 40

Burpees: 25

Sit-ups: 40

Each exercise is followed by 40 sit-ups. Do two rounds or more. Let's see how your fitness has increased.

Warm-down and stretch.

Warm-up and Stretches: Perform light cardio exercises such as jumping jacks or running in place for 5-10 minutes to raise your heart rate and loosen up your muscles. Then, stretch the major muscle groups of your body, such as your hamstrings, quadriceps, chest, shoulders, and back. Hold each stretch for 20-30 seconds.

V-shape push-ups: Assume a push-up position, but with your hands placed closer together than shoulder-width apart and your feet slightly wider than hip-width apart. Lower your chest towards the ground by bending your elbows, keeping them close to your sides. Push yourself back up to the starting position and then walk your hands and feet out to form a V-shape. Repeat for 20 reps.

Sit-ups: Lie on your back with your knees bent and feet flat on the ground. Cross your arms over your chest or place them behind your head. Contract your abdominal muscles and lift your shoulders off the ground until your elbows touch your knees. Lower yourself back down to the starting position and repeat for 40 reps.

Shoulder taps: Assume a push-up position with your hands shoulder-width apart. Lift your right hand off the ground and tap your left shoulder. Lower your right hand back down and then lift your left hand to tap your right shoulder. Repeat for 20 taps.

40 Sit-ups.

Diamond-shaped push-ups: Assume a push-up position with your hands close together, forming a diamond shape with your fingers. Lower your chest towards the ground by bending your elbows and keeping them close to your sides. Push yourself back up to the starting position and repeat for 20 reps.

40 Sit-ups.

Walk-out push-ups: Stand with your feet shoulder-width apart. Bend forward and touch the ground with your hands, then walk your hands out to a push-up position. Perform a push-up and then walk your hands back towards your feet. Stand up straight and repeat for 20 reps.

40 Sit-ups.

Wide-hand push-ups: Assume a push-up position with your hands wider than shoulder-width apart. Lower your chest towards the ground by bending your elbows and keeping them at a 45-degree angle from your body. Push yourself back up to the starting position and repeat for 20 reps.

40 Sit-ups.

Squat thrust push-ups: Stand with your feet shoulder-width apart. Bend down and place your hands on the ground, then jump your feet back to a push-up position. Perform a push-up, then jump your feet back towards your hands and stand up straight. Repeat for 20 reps.

40 Sit-ups.

Mountain climbers: Assume a push-up position with your hands shoulder-width apart. Bring your right knee towards your chest, then quickly switch to bring your left knee towards your chest. Continue alternating for 30 seconds.

40 Sit-ups.

Star jumps: Stand with your feet together and arms at your sides. Jump up and spread your legs and arms out to the sides, forming a star shape in the air. Land softly with your feet back together and repeat for 20 jumps.

40 Sit-ups.

Bear crawl: Start on your hands and knees with your back straight. Lift your knees off the ground and move forward by crawling with your hands and feet. Keep your hips low and crawl for 30 seconds.

40 Sit-ups.

Burpees: Stand with your feet shoulder-width apart. Bend down and place your hands on the ground, then jump your feet back to a push-up position. Perform a push-up, then jump your feet back towards your hands and stand up straight. Jump up with your arms reaching towards the sky. Repeat for 25 reps.

40 Sit-ups.

Warm-down and Stretch: Perform light cardio exercises such as walking or stretching for 5-10 minutes to gradually lower your heart rate and then do some stretches for all the major muscle groups of your body.

Remember to stay hydrated throughout the workout and listen to your body. If you experience any pain or discomfort, stop the exercise and consult a healthcare professional.

Motivation: Environment And Growth

Don't let your environment dictate your future. I tried to grow plants in my home over the years and I could never seem to keep any alive long enough to see them blossom. I wasn't considering things, like the lighting, the position, over-watering, the size of the pot, and love. All these things can affect the growth of the plant. This is no different for you.

Being around the wrong people, doubting yourself, lacking self-confidence, and having low self-esteem are all ways of self-sabotage. Your environment can make you feel incapable. You find it hard to achieve your greatness. Sometimes we don't have any good role models around which can make things even more difficult. Self-belief, a bulletproof mindset and consistency will help you on your journey.

Denzel Washington once said, "Dreams without goals are just dreams and ultimately they fuel disappointment." On the road to achieving your dreams, you must apply discipline but more importantly consistency. Because without commitment you'll never start but without consistency, you'll never finish.

> Your environment does matter,
> plants can't grow in toxic soil.
>
> *- Nicohola Stepheson*

SUPER HEART HEALTH

History

The pomegranate is native to a region from modern-day Iran to northern India. Pomegranates have been cultivated throughout the Middle East, South Asia, and the Mediterranean region for several millennia, and it is also cultivated in the Central Valley of California and in Arizona. Pomegranates may have been domesticated as early as the fifth millennium BC, as they were one of the first fruit trees to be domesticated in the eastern Mediterranean region

Major Benefits

Pomegranates are juicy, sweet fruits with edible seeds called arils packed tightly inside. They're rich in fibre, vitamins, and minerals and even contain some protein. They're also full of antioxidants and anti-inflammatory compounds such as punicalagin. These have been studied for their protective benefits for heart, urinary, brain, digestive, and prostate health. Pomegranate may also have anti-cancer benefits, support exercise endurance, muscle recovery, and fight off harmful germs. Although human research on some of these potential benefits is lacking, it's safe to say that pomegranate is a tasty, nutritious addition to your diet.

Ingredients:

Assorted fruits of your choice (Pomegranate, blueberries and kiwi)

1 tablespoon of honey or agave syrup (optional)

1 tablespoon of freshly squeezed lemon or lime juice (optional)

Mint leaves (optional)

Instructions:

Wash and cut all the fruits into bite-size pieces.

Add the cut fruits into a large mixing bowl.

If you prefer your fruit salad sweeter, drizzle honey or agave syrup over the fruits and gently toss to coat.

If you want your fruit salad to have a tangy flavour, squeeze a tablespoon of lemon or lime juice over the fruits and toss.

If you want to add some extra freshness, tear some mint leaves and sprinkle them over the fruit salad.

Gently toss all the ingredients together until the fruits are evenly coated.

Refrigerate the fruit salad for at least 30 minutes before serving.

Serve the fruit salad chilled and enjoy!

Fitness Session: 15

Target area: Whole-body workout

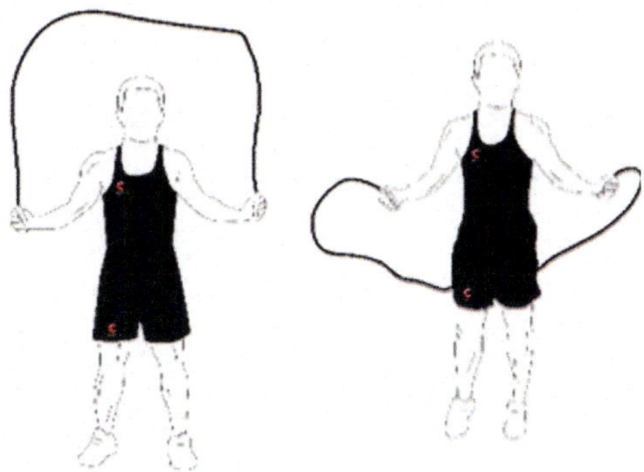

Warm-up then stretches
Minute test: How many can you do?

Push-ups: 1 minute, 30 seconds rest
Burpees: 1 minute, 30 seconds rest
Crunches: 1 minute, 30 seconds rest
Squat with a jump: 1 minute, 30 seconds rest
Mountain climbers: 1 minute, 30 seconds rest
Jumping jacks: 1 minute, 30 seconds rest
V-shape push-ups: 1 minute, 30 seconds rest
Squat thrust: 1 minute, 30 seconds rest
Dips: 1 minute, 30 seconds rest

Warm-down and stretch.

Warm-up and Stretches: This can be any light activity that gets your heart rate up and gets your muscles warm, such as skipping, jogging in place or jumping jacks. Do this for 5-10 minutes. Stretching helps to improve your flexibility and range of motion. You can stretch your major muscle groups such as your legs, arms, back, and neck. Hold each stretch for 10-30 seconds.

Push-ups: Begin in a plank position with your hands shoulder-width apart. Lower your body down by bending your elbows, keeping your back straight, and then push back up to the starting position. Repeat for 1 minute, then rest for 30 seconds.

Burpees: Begin in a standing position, then squat down and place your hands on the ground. Jump your feet back into a plank position, do a push-up, then jump your feet back in and stand up. Repeat for 1 minute, then rest for 30 seconds.

Crunches: Lie on your back with your knees bent and feet flat on the floor. Place your hands behind your head, and lift your shoulders off the ground, keeping your neck relaxed. Lower back down and repeat for 1 minute, then rest for 30 seconds.

Squats with a jump: Stand with your feet shoulder-width apart. Lower your body down into a squat, then jump up explosively as you straighten your legs. Repeat for 1 minute, then rest for 30 seconds.

Mountain climbers: Begin in a plank position with your hands shoulder-width apart. Bring your right knee in towards your chest, then switch to your left knee. Alternate between your right and left knee. Repeat for 1 minute, then rest for 30 seconds.

V-shape push-ups: Start in a plank position with your hands shoulder-width apart on the floor. Open your legs wide so that your body forms a V shape. Lower your body until your chest touches the floor, then push yourself back up to the starting position. Repeat for 1 minute, then rest for 30 seconds.

Squat thrusts: Start standing up, then squat down and place your hands on the floor in front of you. Jump your feet back to a plank position, then quickly jump them back up to your hands and stand up. Repeat for 1 minute, then rest for 30 seconds.

Dips: Sit on the edge of a chair or bench with your hands on the edge and your fingers pointing forward. Lower yourself down by bending your arms, and keeping your elbows close to your sides. Push yourself back up and touch your thumbs together at the top. Repeat for 1 minute, then rest for 30 seconds.

How did you do? Don't forget to warm-down and stretch.

Remember to stay hydrated throughout the workout and listen to your body. If you experience any pain or discomfort, stop the exercise and consult a healthcare professional.

Motivation: Unproductive Days

Unproductive days can lead you miles away from your goals. Every month make a signpost to reflect and start again. This will help you to stay on track with your goals and aspirations. We all have days where we feel unproductive or unmotivated, and these can quickly turn into unproductive weeks or months if we're not careful. By setting up signposts at the end of each month, we can take the time to reflect on our progress and recommit ourselves to our goals.

It is time to sign a contract with yourself in the same way you would sign a contract at work. Nothing happens overnight and these things happen because we don't reflect on ourselves. Also neglecting your goals and not having a plan of action can throw you off-track. So it is key to look back and reflect on your lifestyle and journey.

This practice involves taking stock of our achievements and areas for improvement, acknowledging any setbacks, and reassessing our priorities for the upcoming month. It's a chance to hit the reset button and start fresh, with a renewed sense of purpose and motivation.

Gá

"G.C your love for
the outdoors."

TAKE ON EACH STEP,
THATS HOW GAME CHANGING IS DONE

Don't Give Away Your Power

This book has taken longer than expected, mainly because I gave away my power to someone who I thought had my best interests at heart. When I started this project over a year ago, everything was going according to plan. However, due to my lack of confidence and belief in myself, I handed over the project to a friend. My role was to compile the content, while my friend would organize it all and put everything together. Unfortunately, I soon realised that I had given away my power and control over the project.

As time went by, I found myself constantly reminding my friend of the book's progress and feeling frustrated when he kept telling me what I wanted to hear. This situation led to all kinds of negative emotions, and I felt powerless and frustrated. When we give away our power, we become crippled and powerless. It is crucial to understand that we are the captains of our own ships, and we must not hand over the steering wheel to anyone else.

Despite the signs that our partnership had run its course, I was too blind to see them. However, I now understand that people come into our lives for a season, and it is essential to recognise when that season is over. Even though my journey with my friend had come to an end, I learned a lot from him. We have to focus on the lessons we've learned from people rather than dwelling on the negative aspects. We grow and change as individuals, and people's circumstances also change, leading to different outcomes.

In conclusion, completing this book has taken me out of my comfort zone, forcing me to let go of things that were hindering my progress. But it has also made me realise how gifted I am. With persistence, discipline, and desire, anything is possible. Every storm we go through in life teaches us a lesson, and I am grateful to everyone who has helped me complete this book. We are powerful human beings, and with self-belief, we can achieve anything we set our minds to.

REVIEW ASK

Thank you for reading this book. If you found this book useful, please consider leaving a short review on Amazon to help other readers know what the book is about and how it can help them.

To follow the progression, you can find me on:

Tiktok: @_thagamechanga

Facebook: thagamechanga

Instagram: thagamechanga

ABOUT THE AUTHOR

Horace Jones is a late reader who has experienced a transformative journey through the power of reading. His passion for helping others to succeed in life has led him to focus on three key areas: well-being, mindset, and physical health.

By sharing his personal story, Horace hopes to inspire and encourage readers to believe in themselves and step out of their comfort zones to achieve their own goals. Through the process of writing this book, Horace has learned that anything is possible with dedication and self-belief. He believes that by having more confidence, readers can achieve their dreams and experience the sense of pride and happiness that comes with accomplishing their goals.

This book serves as a testament to the transformative power of self-belief and encourages readers to pursue their passions with confidence and determination.

Printed in Great Britain
by Amazon

32827568R00076